One Foot ir

*A season at the heart c
following Halesowen Town FC*

By Dom Horton

A massive thank you to Phil Passey for the main title, 'One Foot in the Grove' and the front cover photo of me and Kenny.

ISBN: 9798292750994

Imprint: Independently published

© Dominic Horton, 2025.

For:

- Kenny, for being my faithful and enduring companion on the terraces, and
- Lisa, for lovingly putting up with my football obsession.

Contents

		Page
1.	Introduction	4
2.	Pre-season	12
3.	August	15
4.	September	39
5.	October	60
6.	November	77
7.	December	110
8.	January	139
9.	February	161
10.	March	182
11.	April	204
12.	Afterword	228
13.	Statistics 2045/25	231

Introduction

Where should I start? I could start at the very beginning - when I was born. I came into this world on 4 September 1971. It was 6.23am when I emerged. I was obviously excited and could not wait to get out, because it was a Saturday - match day.

But I want to start with a different kind of beginning.

* * * * *

Halesowen Town FC Vs Hitchin Town FC, Saturday 4 November 2023, The Grove Recreation Ground, Halesowen, The Black Country, West Midlands. Southern League Premier Division Central.

It was a miserable day of incessant, heavy rain. From dawn it barely got light until proper darkness descended again shortly before half-time. It was not only a miracle that the game was declared on, but that it was completed. A true testament to the ground staff and their team of willing volunteers. The weather was so bad it knocked a fair few hundred off the gate, which was 721. The average attendance for the season was around 1,200.

My 19-year-old son Kenny and I, Halesowen fans, had opted to stand in the covered Shed End, behind the goal, as opposed to our normal perch on the uncovered East Terrace. Many hardy souls still stood resolutely in the rain in their usual spots, proving the point that most football fans are creatures of habit. Some had hat-less heads, and some even inexplicably wore shorts.

Because besides the biblical rain, it was cold. It was the kind of weather that made you question what you were doing there. But we were there because it's in our blood, in our souls. And in that moment, we did not want to be anywhere else in the world other than a cold, wet, and gloomy Grove Recreation Ground, together, as father and son, bound by our mutual love of football, and of each other.

* * * * *

14 minutes into the game and a long drop kick from Hitchin goalkeeper Charlie Horlock bounced over the head of our otherwise reliable keeper Dan Platt. Despite Platty's best efforts to scramble to ball to safety, it was 1-0 to Hitchin. And this, is the beginning. Why? Well.....

After the goal I said to Kenny that at my first ever Halesowen game, when I was 5, I'm sure the Halesowen keeper scored from a drop kick. It then struck me that was 48 years ago, in 1976 - nearly half a century had elapsed since.

When you turn 40, or 50, people sometimes ask if you feel any different. In my case, the answer was no, I did not. But in that moment of recollection of my first Halesowen Town game, I did have one of those moments, I did feel the passage of time, those 48 years. Those years represent an awful lot of football matches played in and watched, joy and disappointment. But not too many goals where keepers have scored directly from dropkicks.

* * * * *

I was at that Halesowen game as a 5-year-old because I was too young. Me and my older brother by 2 years, Warwick, were taken to watch separate teams with different relatives. Warwick went to watch Aston Villa with my Uncle Albert, and my Grandad Charlie took me to the less bustling Grove to watch Halesowen.

I had to wait another couple of years before I was deemed grown up enough to withstand the rigours of Villa Park. Our Uncle and Grandad took it upon themselves to take Warwick and I to football, because our Dad, Ken, sadly passed away when I was two.

Grandad Charlie took me to watch other local clubs on a Saturday afternoon in those seminal non-League years, like Dudley Town, and Oldbury United. But it was Halesowen Town and the Grove, I was to connect to and return to, from the time I was old enough to go to football without adult supervision.

Warwick did not have those pre-Villa non-League years, so he's never developed the same passion for Halesowen Town FC. But we do go to Villa Park together, with Kenny, and sometimes Warwick's son Charlie. My younger brother, Matt, 7 years my junior, like Warwick, is a Villa fan but does not follow Halesowen. Matt's visits to Villa Park are restricted, as he lives in Dubai.

* * * * *

So, I've held you in suspense long enough. Back to the Yeltz 0 Hitchin 1. If you are wondering who the Yeltz are, well, that's Halesowen's historic and quirky nickname, but more of that later. Did the players rally and lift the gloom of the cold, wet weather? Yes, and, well, no. Popular veteran forward Richard Gregory equalised. 1-1. Then late on in the game we got a penalty. Striker Miracle Okafor, who had scored a whopping 16 goals so far that season, confidently stepped up to take it. And missed.

Then full-back Josh Ezewele's took a throw in back to keeper Platt, and it took a freaky bounce after hitting a divot. It led to Hitchin scoring to make it 2-1. They quickly added a third to make the full-time score 3-1 to them. Kenny and I were frozen to the bone and thoroughly demoralised. It was a dispiriting walk home in the rainy darkness.

In those low moments as a football fan, with the benefit of many years' experience, I tell myself crushing losses like this are valuable investments. Because the ups in football are much better if you experience all the downs. And it made me feel.....no better whatsoever.

* * * * *

In this book I cover the Yeltz's campaign in the 2024/25 season. Us Yeltz fans went into the previous season, 2023/24, full of hope in the Southern League Premier Central, having been promoted from the Northern Premier League Division One Midlands. Under manager Paul Smith the football had generally been easy on the eye. Chairman Keith McKenna, and others behind the scenes, like Yeltz stalwarts Colin and Karen Brookes, had done sterling work and bought the feel-good factor back to the club. So, there was a lot of optimism.

Being a newly promoted club, I think most supporters would have settled for the consolidation of mid-table security. But we got off to a flyer and we quickly found ourselves in the play-off spots, and new striker Miracle Okafor could not stop scoring.

But then around November things got a little sticky. In more ways than one - the pitches got heavier and the free-flowing football that we played earlier in the season suffered, as did our form. There were highlights - we beat our bitter rivals Stourbridge FC home and away, in what is known as the number 9 derby, after the bus route that joins the two towns. But our early season consistency never recovered.

Eventually in February, Paul Smith stood down as manager after results took a turn for the worse, even though we were still in a respectable mid-table position. Former Kidderminster Harriers manager Russ Penn, son of Yeltz FA Vase winning hero Mark Penn, took the reins. Realistically, by this point it would have been difficult for Penn to get us into the play-off positions. But it did give him a good chance to assess the squad ahead of the 2024/25 campaign.

Those early performances under Penn at the tail end of the 2023/24 season were pragmatic and workmanlike. It takes time for a manager to get the best out of players and teams. And the benefit of a full pre-season with a squad cannot be overstated. The old football cliche dictates that pragmatic football is acceptable to fans if success follows. And success to us would mean promotion to the National League North.

* * * * *

For me season 2023/24 was a magical one. There was a lot of grounds for optimism not only for the Yeltz but for my other team too, Aston Villa.

Yeltz were freshly promoted, and Villa were facing European football under Unai Emery for the first time since 2010-11. But the real bonus was that with Villa playing in the Europa Conference League on a Thursday, most of their Premier League games were moved to Sunday. This left Saturdays free to watch the Yeltz. This meant I managed to go to all of Halesowen's home games in all competitions but 2. And Kenny and I went to many away games as well.

My ever-thoughtful son had the decency to split up with his girlfriend early in the season, leaving him footloose and fancy free to watch football with his dear old Dad. Seeing so many Yeltz, Villa, and other games with Kenny over the course of the season was the real magic of it. Saturday afternoon at 3 o'clock we must be in the confines of football stadium watching a game, even if it cannot be Yeltz or Villa.

* * * * *

Where the nickname 'the Yeltz' comes from is a matter of debate and conjuncture. There are different theories, but the truth is nobody knows for sure.

The nickname the Yeltz has long been associated with the club, and was referred to in an 1881 article in the *County Express*. One theory is that Yeltz derives from the old name of the town, Halas. Another is that it comes from a button called 'Yelts' made by the James Grove Button company. Their factory was adjacent to the Grove on the Stourbridge Road from 1866 until 2012.

There are other theories, mainly revolving around the ability of the Black Country accent's tendency to take a word and turn into an entirely different one. Like some think that 'Yeltz' is a corruption of the word 'nails.' Nail making was the town's biggest industry at the time of the formation of the football club.

It is beyond doubt though that the James Grove Button company had a big hand in the history of the club. The club was formed in 1873, and in 1881 it moved to the James Grove Recreation Ground – or the Grove, to give it its short name – on land owned by James Grove, the button factory owner.

In his brilliant book *The Bottom Corner – Hope, Glory, and non-League Football,* Nige Tassell says The Dripping Pan, home of Lewes FC since 1885, is in the top 10 of the oldest football grounds in the country. This must make the Grove in at least the top 9.

The number 9 derby against our near neighbours Stourbridge FC is one of the oldest in the country too, and the oldest surviving one in the West Midlands. The first recorded game took place in November 1880, when Stourbridge were called Stourbridge Standard.

But the likelihood is they have played each other since at least 1877.

It was just over a century later that the highlight of the club's history happened. We won the FA Vase twice at Wembley, in 1984–85 and 1985–86, beating Fleetwood Town and Southall respectively. In 1982-83 we also reached the FA Vase final, losing to VS Rugby, making us the only football team to have played Rugby at Wembley. Paul Joinson was part of the legendary Vase winning teams and he made the most appearances for the club (658) and scored the most goals (368). We have never played in the Football League. You can read more about the club's history in Matt Ponter and Ben Bullock's wonderful book, *Yeltzmen: A History of Halesowen Town Football Club, 1873-2020*.

After rocky times under dubious ownership in the recent past, the club today is in a healthy position. Chairman Keith McKenna, his board of directors, the staff, and volunteers all do a brilliant job to maintain and progress a football club that we are all proud of. So, ahead of the 2024/25 season, I think it's fair to say, Yeltzfolk were very much looking forward to it.

Pre-season

Saturday 13 July 2024, Halesowen Town FC Vs Tamworth FC - Friendly

Tamworth FC were stiff opposition in our first friendly of the new campaign, at a resplendent looking Grove. Last season they were promoted to the National League after winning the National League North.

This was effectively the opening game of the season for me. It came on the eve of England's ill-feted final against Spain in Euro 2024, meaning that there is a certain beauty to one season starting before the last one had ended.

I'm not normally too excited by pre-season friendlies. But with new signings to watch and intermittent sunshine, I was very much looking forward to the match. And 700 odd people must have had similar thoughts, with it being a more than respectable crowd for a friendly.

Even though at most Yeltz games I know several other fans, I do not usually stand with any of them, other than Kenny, or on occasion my best mate Newty, when he comes. That's because during the game I like to dedicate 100% of my focus on it, so I do not like any idle chitchat. When the game is in progress, the only thing I want to talk about is the game itself. If Kenny or Newty do not go to the game, I'd rather usually stand on my own, other than the other select person or two.

But with this being a pre-season friendly, I stood with friends and Jacob and Mike, and I even had a couple of pints with them - a pleasure you can usually enjoy at non-League football grounds. Not something I normally do, as I usually watch football stone, cold sober. But I have to say, I quite enjoyed it for a change. But when the season proper kicks off, I will resolutely revert to type.

It was great to see the lads run out in their royal blue shirts and socks and white shorts. Newbies Ryan Wollacott and Reece Flanagan, defender and midfielder, both signed from Redditch, looked competent. And Conor Tee, from Bromsgrove, excelled in the number 10 position, scoring a wonderful goal in what ended a 2-2 draw. Our star central defender, Ryan Wynter, scored the other.

The signing most Yeltz fans were excited to see was new centre forward Adi Yussuf – a Tanzania international no less - with varied Football League experience. But when he was introduced in the second half there seemed to be an immediate problem - he has chunky thighs, and his shorts clearly did not fit. They looked like they had been sprayed on.

I do not know whether this hampered Yussuf's movement, but he seemed a bit sluggish. But it's early days and I'm sure a few more fitness sessions will sharpen him up and see him gliding past defenders. Or the kit man Nick just needs to get him bigger shorts.

The rest of pre-season – a summary

The overview of the rest of pre-season was that things overall seemed encouraging. But going into the first league game the squad seemed a bit light, especially in forward positions. Adi Yussuf did get off the mark but registered just one goal.

There were good wins against Worcester City and Rugby Town, one step below us in the pyramid. We drew against Hereford and beat Leamington, who are both in the National League North, one step higher than us. We lost 3-0 to National League Solihull Moors, 2 steps higher, and full-time professional, but we put on a good show.

August

Saturday 10 August 2024, Halesowen Town FC Vs Kettering Town FC - Southern League Premier Central

If the thrill of the opening day of the season was not enough on its own, the club has increased the excitement even more by installing a digital electronic scoreboard. This is something of a rarity in Southern League football. So, my fellow Yeltz fans in Roberto's Bar on Thursday night were talking about the scoreboard even more than the club's new signings.

The only problem is that the scoreboard is perched precariously on top of the low-lying Harry Rudge stand, which the ball regularly clears during games. So, unless the screen is suitably protected, we fear this groundbreaking technological development might be short lived. But alas, the ball did not whack the scoreboard during the game, so it lives to fight another day.

Another unusual thing at the Grove for this game was the weather. The opening day of the season brought with it glorious, warm sunshine. Not something ordinarily associated with our wonderful ground, with it being relatively high above sea level. I decided to present Kenny with an early birthday present - the 2022/23 away shirt. It's a retro looking yellow one, with blue pinstripes and a V-neck. A classic. The clement weather would give him a rare opportunity to wear it uncovered. Needless to say, he loved it.

Manager Russ Penn went with the predicted 3 central defenders and 2 wing-backs. But with striker Kieren Donnelly not being properly match fit, he picked 4 midfielders, with only new man Adi Yussuf up top.

Playing with a lone front man seemed to confirm the thoughts of a lot Yeltz fans - that we seem a bit short on attacking options. We do additionally have Boothe and Postle. But the former does not seem to have lots of goals in him, and the latter has lots of potential and talent but he's freshly out of the youth set up. And the squad overall is maybe a little light.

With 1,216 punters basking in the Grove sunshine, and a Yeltz team raring to get stuck into a promotion challenge, the mood was very positive. The game could not have started better - we were on the front foot from the off and after 9 minutes we got a penalty, after Conor Tee was wiped out in the box. New signing Reece Flanagan made no mistake from the spot, and we were off the mark for the season.

Better was to follow 5 minutes before half-time. The magical McKauley Manning, or Mini Macca to us, got the ball onto his left foot from about 16 yards out and hit it to the right of Kettering's keeper. The power was too much. 2-0.

After that the game became tight, and the heat seem to take the sting out of it, which suited us. But on 69 minutes our old foe returned - conceding goals from corners. Dan Javis scored for Kettering, and suddenly it was game on at 2-1.

The scoreboard now became a grim reminder of every excruciating minute left of the game. And to make things worse, Kettering had a series of nerve-jangling corners in stoppage time.

But the referee eventually blew 3 blasts on his whistle, to send the Yeltz fans home happy. And send much needed life back into my body.

I'm not going to be bold enough at this early stage to say things are looking rosy. But at least they are looking as good as the best carnation in an otherwise withered, yellow-stickered, bunch from Tesco Express. The kind I buy my partner Lisa from time to time as an unspoken, thinly veiled, apology for going to too much football.

Prior to the game I like to research the opposition, and it reminded me of a famous football fact. Kettering are the first English football club to have a shirt sponsor, Kettering Tyres in 1976. Former Villa, Wolves, and Northern Ireland striker Derek 'the Doog' Dougan was player-manager at the time, and he did a deal with the firm. But the killjoys at the FA soon put an end to it, saying it was against the rules. But by 1977 the FA relented and allowed shirt sponsorship for all teams.

After the game Kenny and I were in Roberto's Bar, celebrating the win, and catching up on the day's football scores. It was a refreshing day, as there was a full EFL and non-League programme but no Premier League football. So, for once it gave a spotlight to those teams outside the topflight. Into the bar walked a Kettering fan wearing the historic shirt bearing the Kettering Tyres sponsor. Of course, I felt it my duty to say hello, and we had a pleasant chat, as non-League fans do.

As a footnote to the story, I met Derek Dougan as a kid, because he presented me with the trophy for District player of the season when I was 14. He said, "Would you like to be a professional footballer son?" I replied, "Yes, Mr Doogan." And that was that. An encounter almost as brief as the sponsorship of Kettering Tyres on the football club's shirt.

Monday 12 August 2024, Redditch United FC Vs Halesowen Town FC - Southern League Premier Central

Our first local derby of the season quickly followed our opening game on Saturday, and there was a first for me – a long-delayed kick off because of a power cut in the stadium.

Kenny, Newty, and I stood idly basking in the evening sun on the terraces behind a goal, chatting over a pint. We suddenly realised kick-off was drawing near and the players were still on the pitch. And their actions could be more accurately described as milling around than warming up.

It only then struck us that there had been no announcements or music on the Tannoy, and there was no lighting on in the ground. And we had been standing there for over half an hour. We did not even realise there was a power cut when presented with the clues of cold burgers, and the barmaid saying cash only, "Because we have no electricity." Clueless was the word for us. We would not make good detectives.

Time marched on long past the scheduled 7.45 kick off time and fans were in the dark about the game. Not literally, as it was still bright sunshine, but metaphorically, as the Redditch officials could not provide information on the Tannoy. But the game seemed in serious doubt. Darkness descended in the windowless toilets though, and I only knew that I was peeing into the stainless-steel urinals by the sound it was making. Which was a relief in more ways than one.

But the several hundred travelling Yeltz fans seemed undeterred, and the action eventually got underway at 8.40pm on the artificial surface. Plastic pitches are becoming increasingly common in non-League football. Most fans, including me, understand the financial attractiveness of them for clubs at this level. But you cannot beat a grass surface, and I am glad that we still have one at the Grove. And a decent one at that.

To quote a well-worn footballing cliche, this was a game of two halves. First half we played some good football, and we went in at the break 2-1 up. On 8 minutes our goalkeeper Platt made an excellent penalty save from Cameron. This was after our otherwise dependable captain and centre-half Wynter fouled in the box.

But Wynter then quicky made amends on 13 minutes by scoring directly off a corner – shortly after Newty said that's something we never do. Then after the half-hour the sublime Mini Macca dropped his shoulder and put striker Kieren Donnelly clean through. The striker eased the ball over the keeper to make it 2-0. We were in control. Or so we thought.

Instead of going back into the changing rooms, complete with electric lighting, with a clear lead, we conspired to make a game of it by donating Redditch a scruffy goal. Musa Ceesay pulled one back just before the break with a deflected shot, after we failed to clear.

Then an incident before half time set the tempo for what was to follow. One of their players wiped out our right-back Jak Hickman with an extremely high and late challenge. But after consulting both linesmen, and taking a lot of time, the referee only booked the offender and gave cards for dissent to players on both sides.

I have never played the FIFA video game, but if there is a 'local derby' mode I'd imagine it would be like the second half of this match. Tasty, tempestuous, ill-tempered. Oddly set to the background of a beautiful Worcestershire sunset.

The early part of the second half was littered with fouls, petulance, yellow cards, and the referee slowly losing his grip on the game. Kenny said it only seemed a matter of time before someone was sent off, and we hoped that it was not a Yeltzman. But it was, in the unlikely form of Mini Macca. A second yellow card for a silly foul earning him a red on 57 minutes, after being booked for a minor infringement in the first half.

Although the sun was fading, as the game wore on, we felt our hopes of a win was not. We defended stoutly, especially the 3 central defenders of Wollacott,

Wynter, and Kelly. And Redditch offered little attacking threat, right into injury time.

But just when you think it's safe to go back into the water, a draw is snatched from the jaws of a victory. And it was ex-Redditch man Wollacott who was the scorer – a headed own goal. I have never seen a player so crushingly distraught at having beat his own keeper. He had been quite brilliant until that point but was now inconsolable.

But with seconds to go we got a free kick in a threatening area near the corner flag. Up came Wollacott from the back. In the decades of my footballing life, I have never wanted a player to score so desperately. Redditch cleared the corner, but only to Hickman, who put in one of his trademark wonder crosses - outswinger, middle of the goals, head height, decent pace - perfectly onto substitute Boothe's head. Only for the striker to nod it yards over the bar. It was the easiest chance of the game. And I felt absolutely gutted for Ryan Wollacott.

The final whistle blew shortly afterwards, and as the players made their way over to clap us Yeltz fans, and for us to repay the compliment, I noticed Wollacott was missing. In his disappointment he must have gone straight to the changing rooms. A lot of us have had similar experiences in our football careers, and they are very lonely. I wanted to hug him.

I am not much of a social media man but as Kenny drove us back, I hunted Wollacott down on X and sent him a post: "You were brilliant tonight at Redditch, Ryan. Man of the match for me. And great on Saturday too. So, head up mate. Up the Yeltz." Another first for me. He sent me a heart emoji back. Nice to think he had got the message. I hope that it helped.

To complete a hat-trick of firsts, I influenced the referees' actions during the game. He had correctly given Redditch a throw in. But as is custom, the right back had tried to steal at least 10 yards. The referee was standing right by this and took no action. I was so incensed I shouted to the ref to point this out, at the top of my voice, from about 50 yards away. This startled him, and he made the full back retreat to take the throw in. This was greeted by laughter and a round of applause by Yeltz fans in front of us.

I had one of those middle-aged realisations. It is bad enough that I increasingly wrap things up in elastic bands and keep loose change in one of those small plastic bags used by banks. I'm now also a shouty non-League football fan, of the variety that harasses the referee. What next? Will I start taking a Thermos flask to matches?

Saturday 17 August 2024, Halesowen Town FC Vs Bedford Town FC - Southern League Premier Central

Sometimes you can smell a defeat before a ball is even kicked – and this was one of those games.

Nothing in the build up to the game suggested that we would lose. Overall, we did well in a difficult local derby at Redditch, and the manager had a full, if small, squad to pick from. Bedford are freshly promoted from Southern League Division One Central. So, although they would be an unknown quantity, we had no need to fear them at the Grove.

But as we stood there in the sunshine chomping on our burgers before kick-off, I said to Kenny that something does not feel right. I do not know if it was that the crowd was smaller than usual, or there was some sense of apathy in the air. But I had gone from not realising there was a power cut at Redditch on Tuesday, despite the obvious clues, to having an incredible sixth sense. Because we started this game terribly, conceding off a poor free kick after 2 minutes, and in truth never got going after that.

For the rest of the first half, we kept the ball well, while Bedford sat back to protect their lead. But we did not create many clear-cut chances. Even the usually lively Mini Macca was quiet. Mathaius the drummer, in the Shed End behind the goal, was not quiet. But even he had a job lifting the crowd and players to greater things.

Mathaius the drummer is usually positively regarded, bringing colour and atmosphere to games. But that was not the case for Kenny at Mickleover away last season. We stood right next to Mathaius. He was thumping his drum particularly vociferously that day, and it was very loud, with everyone in great voice. After a while, I turned round and looked at Kenny. He was not singing, and he did not seem to be having much fun. "What's up mate?" I asked. "Dad, I'm hungover and that drum is going right through me." Ahhh, that'll be it then.

Back to Bedford. New midfielder Reece Flanagan, who started the season well, sadly dislocated his shoulder, to be replaced by another new man, Ben Cassidy. The latter proving to be our best player on the day.

I was thinking if we get to half time at 1-0 it's not a disaster. The manager, Russ Penn, will tell the players to remain calm and keep playing. He'll say the opposition will tire and it will only be a matter of time before we get a chance, which we will take. Then after that we will go and win the game. But then just before the break, disaster struck. Blake scored a second for Bedford, and the aforementioned team talk went out of the window.

Penn brought on another striker, Adi Yussuf, at half time and reverted to a flat back four. And it was Yussuf who gave us hope by scoring a magnificent header off a Conor Tee cross. But that hope was short lived. Just after the hour Leon Lobjoit scored his second of the game to make it 3-1 to Bedford. And even though there was time left to recover the game, we did not put up much of a fight. To make matters worse, Ryan Blake also scored his second of the game, to make it a comprehensive 4-1 away win for the visitors.

A depressing walk home was only brightened slightly by the news from Kenny that Kidderminster Harriers, who we watch on occasion, had beaten Radcliffe 3-0. I marvel that Kenny can read and navigate his mobile phone, and even send a text message, while walking. Whereas I must stand still, switch to my reading glasses, send the text message, then swap my glasses again. Only then I can proceed to walk.

We were rushing back to watch Villa on the TV. It was a 5.30 kick off away at West Ham in the opening

Premier League fixture of the season. After some Yeltz defeats last season, Villa had cheered us up by winning late kick offs. This was another occasion, Villa coming out 2-1 on top.

One of those times in the last campaign was in Russ Penn's first few games in charge, away at Barwell. Deflated after a dire 1-0 loss, we retreated to the friendly Barwell clubhouse to watch Villa away at Luton. It was notable for two reasons.

The first, was Lucas Digne's dramatic late headed winner in a 3-2 victory for Villa. The second reason was Kenny bumped into Mini Macca in the toilets - not once, but twice. The first time was before the Villa game, and when Kenny told me, I asked what he said to the twinkle-toed midfielder. "Nothing Dad. I think I was a bit starstruck."

The next time was at half-time in the Villa match. "Did you say anything to him this time?" I asked. Ken replied, "I said, 'Not a great game today was it, Macca?', and he said, 'No mate.' And that was that." Not the most riveting of exchanges. But at least Kenny partook in an odd kind of rite of passage that all non-League fans have at some point - talking freely for the first time in a clubhouse with one of your on-field heroes.... or in this case in the toilet.

Monday 19 August 2024. FA Cup first round qualifying draw

At 1pm the Yeltz find out who we get in our first game of this season's FA Cup. It is still the most famous domestic cup competition in the world, and one that holds magical allure for clubs at this level. And in the early rounds, the beauty of the draw is that it's still held on Monday lunchtime, like in the old days. This brings back memories of school, two dozen or so boys hunched over a transistor radio, listening to the draw from FA headquarters at Lancaster Gate.

But as usual, I could not find a radio broadcast covering the draw. BBC Radio 5 had Naga Munchetty handing over to Steffan Powell at 1. He was talking about service stations – surely a subject that is a lot less interesting than the draw for the most famous domestic cup competition in the world. Nothing even on 5 Live Sports Extra. TalkSport as usual had the Jim White and Simon Jordan analysing the Premier League, handing over to Hawksbee and Jacobs at 1. Nothing even on the wonderful Halesowen Town Radio, other than Bob Marley singing 'No woman, no cry'. 'No draw, much cry', would have been more fitting.

Fortunately, a desperate scramble around the internet got me to the Football London website. The good sports there provided live draw updates.

Tie 1 saw giants at this level, Bury drawn away to Garforth Town or Heaton Stannington. The excitement had begun. It seemed somehow more agonising watching ties pop up one by one on a website, compared to listening to them read out loud on the radio.

The FA try to keep fixtures relatively regional in the early rounds of the competition. By tie 22 Midlands teams to start to appear on the screen, with Westfields or Newcastle Town vs Long Eaton. The pressure started to ramp up.

Tie 32 did not help my nerves - Dudley Town vs Stourbridge. Both Black Country teams, and a real local Derby for these parts. Stourbridge are old, bitter rivals, less than 5 miles down the road, with Dudley being a similar distance.

By tie 42 I began to think this might be an anticlimax, and that we could get a bye. What a damp squib that would be. But we were the very next tie out of the hat. And it was spicy - Redditch United vs Halesowen Town.

Hot on the heels of our ill-tempered game just a week ago, it will be back to the Valley Stadium on the 31 August for a second local derby there in quick succession. Let's hope the memorable thing about this game is not the lack of power, but the electric atmosphere.

Saturday 24 August 2024, Halesowen Town FC Vs St Ives Town FC - Southern League Premier Central

This game was the first of the season where there was a clash between Yeltz's and Villa's home fixtures. The former kicked off at 3, and the latter at 5.30. I wished that, like Noel Edmunds, I owned and could pilot a helicopter. I could take off from the grassland at the back of the East Terrace at the Grove at full-time, and land in Aston Park, opposite Villa Park, well before the 5.30 kick-off. But back in the real world, it was a choice between one game or the other.

The latter game won on the basis that although Kenny is a passionate Yeltz fan, he still generally prefers going to Villa Park. And I cannot complain, as after all, that is down to me. When he was 5, I thought I would see if he was able to concentrate on a full 90 minutes of in-stadium football. I thought the allure and razzmatazz of Villa Park would be better than the more sedate surroundings of the Grove. It proved a success, and he was hooked.

Soon after, I took Kenny to the Grove for the first time. He watched the game for a while but then opted to find some boys to play football with down the back of the East Terrace. It was only a £1 for him to get in, so it did not matter. It's still only £2 for under-12's these days. But as he got older, at Yeltz games he played less and watched more.

After the crushing 4-1 defeat to Bedford, I felt mighty guilty not going to this one. I have always been a great believer that you need to support your club in their greatest hours of need. When Villa got relegated to the Championship in 2016 Kenny was only 12, and he said to me, "What happens now Dad?" I replied, "We renew our season tickets and keep coming." Kenny seemed fine with that, as I think he feared I would say we would stop going. He said, "Oh, ok then." He was just happy that we were going to carry on going to Villa Park to support the team, no matter what the division. Which is, of course, the way it should be.

In many ways the game I go to does not really matter, as long as it's with Kenny. Standing on a football terrace with him laughing, shouting, singing, celebrating goals, and politely challenging refereeing decisions, is one of the greatest pleasures of my life.

There was a lot of unnecessary negativity on social media after the Bedford defeat. Maybe Russ Penn could have left a more positive note in his post-match interview. You must be honest as a manager but also take the pressure off the players and give the fans something to feel hopeful about. The interviews are a real skill, and they must be challenging straight after a game.

But on the eve of the match, the mood was lifted with, not 1, not 2, but 3 new signings. Welcome additions, as the general feeling was the squad was light, especially in forward options. And this was not helped by the news that Reece Flanagan would be out for some time with a dislocated shoulder.

The 3 new men being 18-year-old forward Fin Holmes on a one-month loan from National League Solihull Moors, midfielder Josh Smile from Gloucester City, and forward Enock Lusiama, previously of Accrington Stanley, on a short-term deal.

Luckily, Kenny and I could follow most of the game on the way to Villa Park by listening to live commentary on Radio Halesowen Town. It's a brilliant service where commentators Matt Ponter, Frank Williams, and Tom Cartwright run you through the game in skilfully balanced professional but light-hearted way. I'm sure there are not too many teams at this level, or even above, that have a free dedicated commentary of every game. Another reason to be proud to be a Yeltz fan.

It sounded like we were well on top in the first half, with attacking midfielder Conor Tee drawing a string of good saves from St Ives goalkeeper Dan Wilks. And it was Tee who broke the deadlock early in the second half to make it 1-0, which ended up being the full-time score. The highlights on Yeltz TV revealed that Tee's shot took a wicked deflection off a St Ives defender and looped into the net over a hapless Wilks.

But Kenny and I had an agonising wait to confirm that we had won 1-0. Because as full-time drew near in the Yeltz game, we were stuck in an unusually massive queue to get into Villa Park, without a phone signal. The reason for the queue is that Villa have bought in a new app-based season ticket system, and clearly it was not working properly.

Come 5.30 there were still thousands queuing to get in, and they did not delay the kick-off. This is an example of the kind of thing which is making me increasingly alienated from topflight football, and more and more aligned with non-League. At the Yeltz, no fiddly apps, I can either pay £12 by cash or card or rip out a token from my flexi-season ticket book.

But a great win for the Yeltz to get us back on track. In his post-match interview, Penn was delighted with the clean sheet and solid performance. After 4 games we are on 8 points, 3 behind the leaders, Stamford, and 2 behind our bitter rivals Stourbridge, who find themselves in 3rd.

And I have only got to wait until Monday to see the Yeltz again, as it's a bank holiday. And a local derby too, away at Bromsgrove.

Monday 26 August 2024, Bromsgrove Sporting FC Vs Halesowen Town FC - Southern League Premier Central

Even though Bromsgrove is only 8 miles from Halesowen, it was a question of planes, trains, and automobiles to get to the Victoria Ground for the game. Or a bus, two trains, and a 40-minute walk, to be more precise. Well, that was mine and Holly Bush Dave's plan, anyway.

But our plan was foiled. To begin with, the first train we were due to catch from Cradley Heath to Droitwich was cancelled late on because of a lack of drivers. The next scheduled train was running at least half an hour late, because of animals on the line. This a meant a mad dash to the station to catch an earlier train. This culminated in Holly Bush Dave holding the train guard in idle conversation, with him having one foot on the platform and another on the train, until I turned up. I managed to scramble onto the train before the guard ran out of patience with Dave's frivolous chit chat.

But worse was to follow. Bizarrely at Droitwich station there were 2 trains to Birmingham on the 2 different platforms at the same time – one to Birmingham Snow Hill and one to Birmingham New Street. The train we needed was from Droitwich to Birmingham New Street, via Bromsgrove. Unfortunately, we were not giving the situation our full attention. Dave was trying to answer my quiz question of naming the 10 football grounds in England with the biggest capacity outside of the topflight. We jumped on the wrong train and started heading in the opposite direction to Bromsgrove.

We hoped, this was not a sign of things to come, and that by 5 o'clock Yeltz would be heading in the right direction in the table. We got off the train at Kidderminster, and after a quick pint in the delightful King & Castle at the station, decided to get a taxi to Bromsgrove. Which at least meant we did not have to take the 40-minute walk at the other end.

Holly Bush Dave was my sole companion, with Kenny being on holiday in Dorset. Dave's an old friend and the 'Holly Bush' bit comes from the fact that he owns, lives in, and runs a pub of the same name. I say 'pub' - it kind of is, and is not, a public house. Dave opens it when he wants, and runs it how he wants, and basically lets in who he wants. Like Dave himself, it's quite an eccentric affair.

I once wrote and acted in play with Dave at the Holly Bush, as it's an arts venue as much as a pub. Dave and I were in the lead roles. Even though Dave had prior acting experience, his performances in rehearsals left a lot to be desired. But he assured me everything would be alright on the night.

Having not acted before, I sought advice from a thespian friend of mine, Pete the Tongue. One of his nuggets of wisdom was, "Do not have more than one pint before the show." In the build up to the opening curtains, I was observing Dave behind the bar, and he had at least 5 or 6. I thought to myself, we are going to die on our arses. Which was ironic, as the play was about suicide. But incredibly, he was word perfect, he got all his cues, and his delivery was spot on. And the play went down as well as the 6 pints Dave had before the show.

When we finally got to the Victoria Ground, as usual it looked absolutely resplendent. The pitch was perfect, and it's one of the finer grounds in non-League football. As expected, hundreds of Yeltz fans had made the short journey and were in fine spirits in the sunshine, including many friends and familiar faces making up the 1,310 crowd. The scene was set for a mouth-watering local derby. And to add to the mix, ex-Yeltz gaffer Paul Smith is now the boss of Bromsgrove.

The game started in a typically combative local derby style, with our new diminutive, but competitive, midfield man, Josh Smile, looking the part. Not just a tackler, but a ball player too. He made a great pair with Todd Parker, who has fantastic passing ranges with both feet, and has a knack of winning the ball back without needing to tackle.

Despite us looking relatively comfortable, it was the home side who took the lead on 19 minutes when Charlie Wragg was sent clean through. He made no mistake by slotting the ball cooly past Platty.

But we only had to wait 3 minutes for the reply, when our forward Kieren Donnelly finished neatly after some good footwork in the box. 1-1. After that we seemed the better team. But we could not have anticipated the treat that was to come.

With 10 minutes to half time, following a corner, the ball dropped to central defender Nat Kelly, about 20 yards out. The left footed stopper is not known for his goalscoring prowess, but he fancied a shot and put his boot through it - and it absolutely rocketed, curling outwards, right into the top corner.... an absolute belter!!! While jumping on me Dave screamed "NAT KING GOAL!!!"

It was particularly pleasing because Kelly, a former player who was re-signed this season, is a rugged, head it, kick it, no nonsense, reliable, unassuming, central defender. He just gets on with it. He did not even really celebrate the goal. He just stood there and smiled. What a bloke!

The second half was thankfully largely uneventful, except for a lot of local derby huff and puff, with loanee sub Fin Holmes providing some brightness. Considering defending corners is our Achilles heel, a late flurry of them in Bromsgrove's flavour was difficult to endure. Yeltz Matchday Announcer Paul Essom, who stood in front of me, could barely watch. But we hung on to secure a 2-1 win. It was a delicious victory to celebrate with the players and staff in front of us, in the glorious Worcestershire sunshine.

The win takes us up to 5th, on 10 points, in the play-off places. But with Stourbridge somehow winning again, they remain 2nd on 12 points, with Stamford still leading on 13. Only one gets promoted automatically, with the next 4 going into the play-offs.

Our journey home was more straightforward. Dave managed to cadge us a lift off his mate John, who like Dave and I, is also a Villa fan, and obviously a Yeltz fan.

So, we had a pleasant journey home, talking about our clubs.

We set ourselves in the Wetherspoons in Halesowen, the William Shenstone. Dave displayed one of his many eccentricities, by covering his meal in most of the condiments on offer. In his world, a mixture of ketchup and mustard is perfectly normal.

Another one of his quirky traits is that he likes to set you a football quiz challenge. Nothing odd with that you might think. An example might be, "Name Aston Villa's top 10 scorers in the Premier League era." But it quickly becomes apparent that he does not know the answers himself. And when you start to run out of ideas, he does not want you to Google things either. This can lead to long, drawn-out quiz challenges that last a few days over text messages until they are complete. By which time Dave will have just about digested the revolting mix of ketchup and mustard.

Saturday 31 August 2024, Redditch United FC Vs Halesowen Town FC - FA Cup 1st round qualifying

Our run in the most famous domestic cup competition in the world this season was confined to one game. And overall, it was a dismal affair.

In recent history our relationship with the FA Cup has not been a very good one. I stood with Lee in the first half, and he rightly said that the last time we got to the 1st round proper was many years ago when we lost to Yeading. How long ago was that he wondered? 20 years, I said with great confidence, because it was the year that Kenny was born.

Getting to the 1ˢᵗ round proper is the Holy Grail for non-League teams like us, because that's where lower division Football League teams enter the competition. So, for the Yeltz, it could mean a chance of knocking out a League team at a packed Grove, or an away day at the likes of on-trend Wrexham, or a local derby at fellow Black Country team Walsall. The 3ʳᵈ round, played in January, is fairy tale land, because that's when you have a chance of drawing a team from the Premier League.

As a fan of a non-League team, or even a lower league EFL team, you know you have no chance of winning the FA Cup. But every year it brings glamour and the excitement of potentially going on a run - I would imagine it's a baffling concept to our American cousins. It also brings the possibility of bringing in a few pennies into the coffers.

You will remember the board approved the signing of 3 players that Penn brought in before the St Ives game. So, I'm sure he felt some extra pressure to win this fixture for the financial reward, as much as the footballing glory.

Kenny chose to watch Villa, who were kicking off at the same time at Leicester. So, it was another bus and train journey to Redditch. It seemed a simple trip.

Arriving at Birmingham New Street, the board on the platform said 13.15 to Redditch. But when I got on the train, the electronic display said 'train to Four Oaks' - which is in the opposite direction. Determined not to have another train disaster, I asked for clarification from fellow passengers, but they did not seem confident.

The train doors beeped, signalling imminent departure, and my rising sense of panic. I opened the doors and looked around the platform for an official, but there was none to be seen. So, determined that the train was not going to leave until I knew its true destination, I took the only course of action open to me - I put one foot on the platform and another on the train.

From the other end of the platform, 6 carriages away, I heard a loud shout from the train guard: "Oi! What are you doing?!!" Just at that moment an official in a high vis jacket popped up from the escalator. I asked if this was the train to Redditch, to continued abusive shouting from the train guard in the background. The official said it was. I asked why the display said it is the train to Four Oaks. She said, "Oh, it often says that." The display said train to Four Oaks for the entire journey.

Inside the Valley Stadium my pre-match burger was again stone cold. So, the cold one I was served a couple of weeks ago had nothing to do with the power cut after all. And £6 for the privilege, a tidy price for a non-League football ground in the Midlands.

The first half was forgettable. We defended well, but so did they. Our only real quality came from the impressive Josh Smile in midfield, and the fleet-footed Mini Macca at left wing back. Then, just before half time, Redditch kindly donated us a goal. Their keeper Dale Eve seemed to misjudge the bounce of the ball on their plastic pitch, and Kieran Donnelly headed into an empty net.

But Redditch quickly took control of the game after the break. Our defence was twice caught colder than the snack bar's burgers. Jaiden White ran through both times to score a brace. Worse was to follow with 20 minutes to go, and our old Achilles heel caught us out again - defending corners. Johnston headed in unmarked to make it 3-1 to them.

Any hopes of a comeback were finally quashed on 82 minutes when substitute Adi Yussuf was sent off. And despite Donnelly's 96th minute consolation, there would be no FA Cup trip to Wembley this year – or Wrexham, Walsall, or anywhere else.

September

Saturday 7 September 2024, Halesowen Town FC Vs Leiston FC - Southern League Premier Central

It's seemed like a long week, following the bitter FA Cup defeat to Redditch. But there was every cause for optimism for a home win, with Leiston having only taken 5 points from their opening 5 league games. And with few top 4 division games, because of the international break, a bumper 1,203 crowd was inside the Grove to cheer the Yeltz on.

I needed a win to cheer me up. Because in the week I'd done the most middle-aged thing of my life yet, without even thinking about it, until a sad realisation later. I redeemed a £25 Amazon gift voucher, I had for my birthday, on a large tub of weedkiller.

My mate Phil was up from London to accompany Kenny and I on the terraces. I met him many years ago, when we both worked in a petrol station as teenagers, starting on £1 an hour. This was long before the introduction of the minimum wage. Despite the paltry pay, I felt like a rich man as it was my first proper job, beyond being a paper boy. And our wages were supplemented by several unofficial sidelines. They were orchestrated by the manager, a frustrated fisherman from Dorset, who looked like Billy Boswell from the sitcom *Bread*.

I mentioned to Phil that I'm writing a book about following the Yeltz this season, and he asked what the title is. I said I do not have one currently, because I'm thinking the ultimate outcome of the season might shape the title. But he quickly came up with *One Foot in the Grove*. I said it's good, but it makes me sound like I'm on the point of croaking, or some footballing Victor Meldrew. But the more I think about it, the more I like it. So, if it does end up being the title of this book, credit to Phil.

Phil is a a boyhood Yeltz fan who was at Wembley. Work took him South and having edited Beckenham Town's programme for four years, he's now similarly involved with Dulwich Hamlet. When it comes to the Grove, he likes to get to the ground at 1pm, take in the atmosphere, meet up with old players, go to the club shop, and take lots of photographs. He took some very fetching pictures of the back of mine and Kenny's heads. You would have to see them to appreciate their artistic qualities.

In the first half of the game there was not a lot of artistic qualities on show, other than from the magical left foot of Mini Macca. He had been moved into midfield, with Todd Parker feeling the manager's axe after Redditch. The other change saw new man Enoch Luisiana come in at centre forward for the suspended Yussuf. It was fair to say Yeltz had the best of the first 45, but the quality of the football fell far short of entertaining.

But the second half started with a bang. Just when we were debating whether Luisiana would be the answer to our number 9 issues, he came up with a goal - and a good one too, an overhead kick after Leiston failed to clear, following a corner. 1-0.

Donnelly missed a golden chance shortly after, but we then failed to push sufficiently for a second goal to kill the game off. And what I could sense was coming then materialised – a Leiston equaliser. On 84 minutes Clements scored to draw the visitors level. 1-1.

We huffed and puffed after that, and we should have got the winner, hitting the woodwork twice and drawing several saves from their keeper, Johnson. But in truth, we did not attack the opposition enough, who were there for the taking, and we played disjointed football.

The point leaves us 6th, and although we are only 2 points behind the leaders – wait for it - Stourbridge, the mood music does not seem quite right somehow. The team is short of being cohesive, and unless Yussuf or Luisiana come good quickly, we clearly lack a centre forward who is going to lead the line, and bag us sufficient goals. But equally, we do not seem too far off either.

The rest of September could be critical. We travel to Banbury on Tuesday, then to Alvechurch on Saturday, before 3 home games against Hitchin, Harborough, and Stratford. Whatever happens, we cannot let Stourbridge run away from us.

Tuesday 10 September, Banbury United FC Vs Halesowen Town FC - Southern League Premier Central

A few weeks ago, I got disproportionately excited about the prospect of going to this fixture. This was because I sniffed out return train tickets for the meagre sum of £9.50. Before booking the tickets, I was about to text Kenny to see if he wanted to go. It was only then

I realised that I could not go myself, because I was due to go on holiday with Lisa to Winchester.

So, I will not be going to Banbury on a cock horse. Or Virgin trains, or any other means of transport.

For my Christmas present, Lisa had sportingly arranged tickets for the England v Australia T20 cricket international at Southampton. So, we decided to base ourselves in Winchester and make a small break of it. At that stage, during the middle of last season, we could not have known that Yeltz would be playing at Banbury at the same time. If I had known, I could have tried to spin it in my favour with a line like, "I hear Banbury is magical in September love."

Teasingly the train to Winchester from Birmingham took us through Banbury. I even got a glimpse of the ground, leaving me with thoughts of what could have been. But despite England losing to the Aussies by 28 runs, the T20 cricket at the Utilita was a fantastic spectacle. It was effectively won by a world class batting display by Travis Head, who smashed 59 from 23 balls.

Before the Yeltz game, it was a hard one to gauge. The draw against Leiston felt like a defeat. But after 7 games we were 3rd in the table on 14 points, so averaging 2 a game - only 2 points behind the leaders Stamford. On the face of it, a good start. But it feels like there is more to come. Banbury had started well, and it is a tough place to go.

The headline from the team news was that 40-year-old reserve goalkeeper, and goalkeeping coach, Lewis

Solly, is in to replace Yeltz stalwart Dan Platt. He has a stomach illness.

When the game was in progress I was in a restaurant, then a pub, with Lisa. So, I could not listen to the commentary on Halesowen Town Radio. So, I had to follow the game by now and again surreptitiously dipping into the updates on X. Which is about anxiety inducing as being drip fed information when a family member is being held hostage by terrorists. I'd imagine.

The story of the game seems to be that it was pretty tight, both teams had chances, us have the better of them. And substitute Ryan Boothe converted one of them on the 81st minute from close range, following an uncleared corner. The goal was the only one of the game, securing a 1-0 win and 3 points for the Yeltz.

In his match report on the club website, David Johnson called it the 'best performance of the season to date.' A clean sheet for Solly. But despite pressure from Banbury at times, people who went to the game told me that he was never seriously troubled. The highlights on Banbury United YouTube channel seemed to bear this up.

Undoubtedly a fantastic result, taking us to 3rd in the table. Onwards to Alvechurch on Saturday.

Saturday 14 September 2024, Alvechurch FC Vs Halesowen Town FC - Southern League Premier Central

Today holds a thrilling and rare prospect - watching both Yeltz's and Villa's games on the same day.

The Yeltz game kicks off at 3 at Alvechurch, with Villa's at 5.30 at Villa Park. Getting to Alvechurch, in rural Worcestershire, from my home in Halesowen is pretty straightforward – a bus 8 odd miles into Birmingham City centre, then a train to Alvechurch and a pleasant 15-minute stroll to finish. But getting from Lye Meadow to Villa Park poses more of a *Challenge Anneka* problem.

It's just over 13 miles from one ground to the other. I did not expect the Yeltz game to end until about 5. That only leaves 30 minutes before kick-off in the Villa game, which rules out the train. Kenny was meeting me at Villa Park. But even if he had drove to Alvechurch then on to Villa Park, the 20-minute walk from the car park at the other end would have scuppered us. And it's about a 45-minute drive, taking traffic into account.

So, the only option was to pre-book an Uber taxi, something I had never done before. It meant missing the first 15 minutes of the Villa game, but it was the best I could do. Pre-booking the Uber was simple enough but scary, as I was completely reliant upon the taxi turning up as agreed. But like football itself, the jeopardy added to the excitement.

Once off the train at Alvechurch, I ambled through sleepy country lanes in the autumn sun thinking of the game. A week is definitely a long time in football. The lethargy following the Leiston draw has given way to the heady prospect of topping the league if we win today and results go our way. But it will not be easy as Alvechurch have started well, and are only a point behind us, 5th in the league.

Alvechurch's Lye Meadow ground is one of the most picturesque in Midlands non-League football, with sheep filled rolling hills as a backdrop. It represents one of the finest days in my long amateur playing career. I was wearing the colours of Handrahan Timbers FC, who before you ask are not a North American Soccer League team from the 70s. We beat them 4-3 in the cup, in a breathtaking game, when they were a league higher.

Alvechurch have since pushed on a couple of divisions. And I have become a middle-aged spectator with a flat cap, glasses and a stick, reduced to writing about the quality of burgers at non-League football grounds. For the record, the burgers at Alvechurch were not bad. Before the game, Holly Bush Dave had 2. And a portion of curry sauce and chips. All splattered in a plethora of condiments, as usual.

One of the songs us Yeltzfolk sing is *Oh, What a Beautiful Mornin'* from the musical *Oklahoma*. The opening line is "There's a bright golden haze on the meadow." During this fixture last season, I took a fetching photo of the ground, with the hills in the background. I posted it on a Yeltz Facebook feed with the caption, "There's a bright golden haze on Lye Meadow." Disappointingly, it got no likes. Or comments. Not even by the following Saturday.

After Solly's clean sheet at Banbury, Penn retained him in the sticks, despite long time first choice keeper Platty being back in the fold. He was on the bench. Boothe was bought in up front after his late goal on Tuesday, at the expense of Luisiana. This was much to the dissatisfaction of the many Yeltzfolk I spoke to before the game.

The early part of the game was frenetic, mostly percentage play, with the ball leaving the turf too often for most fans liking. Everyone hoped that the contest would break out into game of football. But as the half wore on, it was clear that was not going to happen. Yeltz did have the better of the first 45 minutes, with the industrious Donnelly having some half chances. But there was nothing clear cut.

And things only got worse in the second half, when we failed to establish any sustained pressure on their goal. With defences on top, it was looking like a goalless draw was the best we could hope for. But more the fool me for being so optimistic. Because on 84 minutes Alvechurch sub Dan Shaw curled one from 25 yards that sailed over Solly, into the corner of the net.

At the other end, Boothe was very poor. Yeltzfolk's objections to him are less about his quality, but more due to his apparent lack of effort and aggression. The manager succumbed to the inevitable on 65 minutes and replaced Boothe with Luisiana. On his retreat to the Yeltz dugout Boothe had to walk the gauntlet of Yeltz fans behind the goal. There were no claps for him, and it was a mixture of tumbleweed and the old boo and disparaging comment. And no doubt a multitude of private thoughts of, "What on earth does the manager see in him?"

A solid Alvechurch held out, and their 1-0 win saw them take top spot in the table. In his post-match interview on Yeltz TV Penn said, "I don't think it was a very good game at all to be honest, you couldn't believe they've gone top of the league today watching that." But as the cliche goes, the league table does not lie.

A defeat always leaves a bad taste in the mouth. But we lost by the odd goal in a game of fine margins, to a decent outfit. We are still doing well in the league, 4th, two points behind the leaders Stamford, and one place ahead of Stourbridge. But it does leave me wondering if that fine margin might have swung in our favour, if Fin Holmes, or Lusiana, had started over Boothe.

But was my Uber waiting? Yes! And it whisked me away to the most wonderful game of football at Villa Park, that saw us go 2-0 down to Everton, only to fight back to win 3-2. And the winner was a goal of the season contender from sub Jhon Durán. I love it when a plan comes together.

Saturday 21 September 2024, Halesowen Town FC Vs Hitchin Town FC - Southern League Premier Central

After last week's bitter defeat at Alvechurch I was Hitchin to get to this game, to hopefully see the Yeltz win. Which we should have done, as the Canaries started the day bottom of the table with no points, scoring only 6 and conceding 20. Obviously, in football victory is never a foregone conclusion.

Hitchin are the original Canaries, having been founded in 1865, with Norwich City FC being founded in 1902. Not something you hear Delia Smith cooking up a fuss about.

But Villa were at home at 3 o'clock too, and to local rivals Wolves. So, Kenny and I went to Villa Park. I paid £600+ for my season ticket, so I need to make the most of it, and Kenny preferred to go to the Villa game too. The other spin is that Yeltz are at home versus Harborough on Tuesday, with Villa being away to Wycombe in the League Cup. So, we will go to the Grove, in preference to watching the latter game on TV.

So, I could not even enjoy the commentary of Matt Ponter, Frank Williams, and Tom Cartwright on Halesowen Town Radio today. Match updates were limited to team news, and half-time, and full-time updates on X.

Those updates left me with utter disbelief. Yeltz were 2-0 down at half-time and conceded a woeful 4 without reply by full-time. I searched the X updates to see how many men Yeltz had sent off, because surely that was partly the reason for the dismal result. But the answer was none. What on earth had gone on at the Grove?

When I do not go to a Yeltz game, it's a case of piecing together what happened over the forthcoming days, like a detective. Listening to eyewitness accounts - mostly in the pub - scouring social media comments, reading match reports, listening to commentary playbacks, watching highlights, and the gaffer's post-match interview.

The result of my extensive investigations was that we were truly awful, pretty much from start to finish. Both going forward and defending. As you can imagine, although social media comments were varied, they all had a common theme - they were scathing.

An old rule dictates that if you do not go to the game, you are not entitled to comment on it. And I do not intend to break that rule. The fabled sports show host Tony Butler had a post-match phone in on a Saturday on the old Midlands radio station BRMB. Fans would call in and start spouting their opinions on a game. "Have you been to the match?" Tony would ask. If the answer was no, he would have short shrift with the caller, and the executioner's axe would fall with his words, "On yer bike!!!" And he would hastily cut them off. And rightly so.

In the pub on Sunday night, my mate Ade confirmed how bad the performance was. We do not normally talk too extensively about the game, because the women present do not like football. So, being modern men (!) we aim for inclusive chat. But this game needed full analysis and dissection. Ade had my full attention for two whole pints, and it could have gone on until closing.

In the post-match interview on Yeltz TV, manager Russ Penn looked understandably shell-shocked. I felt for him, because nobody feels the ill effects of a poor result more keenly than the manager. He has probably not felt so down too many times in his football career. But it's also part of being in charge.

Although he apologised for the result, Penn made it clear that mainly the players should take the responsibility for it. He questioned the attitude of some, who he did not name. In a post-match interview, it can be a fine balance between being honest and throwing the players under the bus. If you are not careful, you can lose the players' respect and ultimately the dressing room. But sometimes the manager is right to call out the players.

The defeat leaves us in 6th place, outside of the play-off places, and 5 points behind leaders Stamford. But still ahead of local rivals Stourbridge, who also lost.

There's no time to lick wounds and take stock, with the impending home game on Tuesday. It seems unfair to say it could be a pivotal game, but that might be the case. If we win, we will be back on track and hopefully back in the play-off places. But a loss, the 3rd in a row, might see pressure mounting on Penn, and you know what modern football is like.

Villa beat Wolves 3-1. In another post-interview talking point, in referencing to his own team's first half performance, manager Unai Emery used the word sh*t. It was tastefully bleeped out on *Match of the Day*. It must have taken Russ Penn all his steely resolve not to use a similar word in his.

Monday 23 September 2024. FA Trophy 3rd round qualifier draw

Today I realised I have unwittingly developed another middle-aged habit, that I caught myself doing on a visit to the barbers. After I've had my hair cut, I pay Joey, the barber, by card but then for some reason pay him a £1 tip in cash. I do this after he has beautifully finished off my hair, and I ruin it by plonking on my flat cap. Joey is younger than me by over 2 decades, and my parting gift of a £1, invariably in the form of two 50p's, is almost like me saying, "There we go lad, buy yourself some sweets." Despite Joey being a family man in his 30's. It needs to stop.

Anyway, after Saturday's debacle all Yeltzfolk were hoping for an exciting FA Trophy draw to look forward to. But what come out of the hat was an uninspiring boomerang fixture...... Redditch away – again.

Tuesday 24 September 2024, Halesowen Town FC Vs Harborough Town FC - Southern League Premier Central

I sat in the splendid King Edward VII pub, next to the Grove, with Kenny and Newty, enjoying a luscious pint of Oakham Bishop's Farewell. I contemplated the game ahead. For me, drinking real ale has not come to me in middle age. It's always been my beer of choice, since I started supping. In our little corner of the Black Country, we have always been rich in cask ale, even in the lean years of the 80's, when I was a teenager.

I was not sure how to feel before this game. Normally it's simply a question of pure excitement. But after

Saturday, I have an understandable sense of twitchiness. And this is heightened by a sense of empathy for the gaffer, who would have been through the emotional wringer. So, I'm guessing he will have some nerves before tonight too.

If we lose, 3 defeats on the spin are not good for the manager. And an outwardly nervous manager is not good for the players, because it can rub off on them and affect their performance. Question is, can the gaffer turn those nerves into passion and drive and inspire and motivate the players? That's the test for tonight, and I was hoping he passes it with full marks.

The answer to the question started to become evident quite early in the contest. Clearly, Penn had got the desired reaction out of the players, because we were on the front foot, passing was crisp, and movements were sharp. We were getting at the opposition, and that got the crowd – albeit it unusually small 615 – behind the team.

And it did not take long to get a breakthrough. Harborough cleared a corner, but the ball was helped back into the box. The ever-alert Keiren Donnelly was on hand to tuck it into the net from close range. Which was just what was required following Saturday's result. 1-0 to the Yeltz.

Donnelly was playing as a lone centre-forward. Big summer signing Adi Yusuf was dropped to the bench, following an apparently poor performance on Saturday. I hear Enoch Luisiana has decided to end his single goal spell at the club after not starting on Saturday. And Fin Holmes returns to Solihull Moors after tonight's game following his loan spell. Leaving our striking options depleted.

We continued to be the best team in the first half. But after the break Harborough made changes that made the difference. The game was more even, tense, and keenly contested. Both teams had half-chances, until midway through the second half.

Then Mini Macca found himself one-on-one with their keeper, and predictably he danced round him. There was one player on the line, but all the sure-footed Manning had to do was roll it into the net for a 2-0 lead. But he somehow managed to hit the defender, and the chance was lost.

Then things got increasingly tense. Harborough pushed and added pressure. Platty pulled out saves, skipper Ryan Wynter was gigantic. Time crawled slowly on, until eventually the scoreboard showed 90 minutes. But the referee, who was excellent, added on another 6 minutes for us to endure. But endure the players did, and 3 very hard-earned points were secured.

The win not only changes the entire mood but leaves us in 4th spot, only 2 points behind leaders Stamford. It also led mine, Kenny's and Newty's happy legs to Roberto's Bar without our brains telling them to go there. Our arms then hoisted pints of beer to our lips on autopilot, while we rejoiced about the game.

On to Stratford at home on Saturday. A new script waiting to be written.

Saturday 28 September 2024, Halesowen Town FC Vs Stratford Town FC - Southern League Premier Central

Occasionally on a Saturday, I arrive at the Grove on my own before the game. This week, Kenny was meeting me there. I got chats out of the way with Yeltzers I know with 20 minutes remaining before kick-off.

I took my regular spot on the East Terrace and took great pleasure in taking in the scene. To my left, fans filtered in from turnstiles behind the Stourbridge Road Terrace. Some coming from that direction will leave it until the last minute, piling in from the adjacent King Edward VII pub. For the few games away fans are segregated, they are placed in the Stourbridge Road Terrace. Other than that, supporters are free to stand or sit where they please.

Most of the fans who enter from the Stourbridge Road turnstiles walk across the top of the East Terrace, heading towards the action - the corner of the East Terrace and the Shed End, behind the goal to my right. This corner hosts the entrance to the Shed End, the James Grove Lounge, the well-stocked club shop, and the main toilets. And the catering hut is not far away either. Fans converge there too from the Old Hawne Lane turnstiles, making it a hive of activity and noise before kick-off.

Directly opposite me is the Harry Rudge stand, the only seated area in the ground. Harry, or H, was a club legend, Mr Halesowen Town, who for decades undertook every conceivable role at the club. My friend John is Harry's nephew. He told me H used to say that life is what happens while you are waiting for 3 o'clock on a Saturday to come round again. And it is a saying that definitely strikes a chord with me.

In the corner of the Harry Rudge stand and the Shed, is the smaller Harry's Bar. Some like to stand there and watch the game, with easy access to the bar. Almost like they have found a secret way to cheat the queues at the James Grove Lounge.

It was the perfect day to play football. Overcast, minimal breeze, slight crispness in the air. The kind of day that as a player you are lucky enough to get once or twice a season. The ground was filling up nicely, and the eventual crowd was back to normal, at 1,001.

I watched the players warming up to give me clues about the mood of the camp, and how that might affect the outcome of the game. Today I especially had my eye on sub Jordan Ponticelli, a striker the club signed yesterday. The 26-year-old former Kings Lynn Town man, has previous played for Coventry City and Wrexham, so is an exciting and much needed addition to the squad. And we all hoped he would get on the pitch today. Following Tuesday's win, Penn has backed the same starting 11, which is fair enough.

This part of the proceedings, just before the game, is always a treat. The sights, the smells, the sounds. Some fans scurry around to get a pint or some food, visit the toilet, or towards their preferred spot. Others are already in place for the match, and chatter excitedly about the game, or other things. Being inside a ground just before kick-off on a Saturday afternoon is an indescribable feeling. In many ways, it's a big part of what I live for.

I know none of us live forever. But I still cannot comprehend that Saturday afternoons will go on without me being in a stadium watching a game of football somewhere, somehow, forever. I'm not ready to make sense of that yet. Maybe I never will.

Sometimes a game of football can be defined by a moment - this was one of them. Yeltz centre-back and skipper Ryan Wynter joined the club at the start of season 2023–24. From day one he's been rock steady and reliable, sure footed on the ball, and a defensive colossus. One of the best signings the club has ever made. But even the best players make mistakes. And at 2-1 to the Yeltz, with 5 minutes to go, and us looking good for the win, Wynter hesitated on the ball, instead of clearing. This allowed Stratford forward Reece Scythe to dispossess him. Styche then stroked the ball past Platt to level the scores 2-2.

At that point, I was more gutted for Ryan Wynter than anything else because, it was the first foot he had put wrong in the game. And I knew he would take it hard that he had cost us 2 points. But that was not the case - because we also decided to throw away the point we had left. We failed to clear, leading to a scramble that Lewis Wilson converted for Stratford. It gave them a last-minute, gut-wrenching winner, and we lost 3-2.

To the casual observer of the sport, to say a game can be defined by a moment might seem odd. After all, it's only a split second, and there are 22 players on the pitch at any one time. But football fans will know what I mean.

A lot of social media comments were not favourable, some about the style of football, some about Russ Penn. One fan even verbally accosted him by the dugout at the final whistle. Penn tried to reason with the fan. All the criticism of Penn today seems a bit harsh.

Firstly, overall, we played pretty well. The teams were evenly matched, but we took the lead on 37 minutes through Conor Tee after Todd Parker poached the ball off a Stratford player on the edge of the box. We allowed them an equalise, to make the score 1-1, just before the break. We failed to mark Ebanks, who headed in freely off a cross.

Secondly, the manager gambled with an attacking change at a critical stage in the game, which proved successful. On the hour he bought on Jordan Ponticelli, to partner Keiren Donnelly, as an additional forward. Shortly after, Ponticelli produced a spectacular overhead kick, that their keeper just clawed out. KD pounced on it, to score and send us 2-1 up. Credit to the gaffer, and it should not go unnoticed.

Credit also for right wing-back Jak Hickman for the incredible cross that led to that goal. Hicky's ability to whip in in-swinging balls from the right is unparalleled at this level, often on the run. He puts many professionals to shame, especially as in the higher reaches of the sport crossing seems to have gone out of fashion. And he's an object example of you do not need to beat the defender to cross the ball, à la John Robertson or Chris Waddle.

You can look at this game two ways - Wynter clears the ball, and we win the game 2-1. Or Penn was brought in on a ticket of clean sheets and solid wins, but we have conceded 3 silly goals again, leading to a 3-2 defeat. My view is the former prevails, but we do need to stop conceding easily preventable goals.

Kenny and I shelved our plan of heading straight home to watch the 5.30 game on TV, to ease our sorrows in Roberto's Bar. We were speechless by the dreadful ending to the game and just wanted to wallow in our miseries. I was hoping that fellow Yeltzers Sid and Kev would be in there too, so we could form an impromptu support group.

But instead, we were greeted by John from the band we are both in, the Shambolics. He's not a really a football fan. He was full of the joys of spring because of an uplifting gig he played in the night before, with another band he's in. On the one hand it was welcome, as it dragged our thoughts from the trauma that had just befallen us. On the other, there's nothing more annoying than someone being jolly when you have just experienced a last-minute defeat.

The defeat leaves us 5th in the table, 2 points behind Stamford, who have a game in hand. In a bizarre plot twist Stamford have signed ex-Yeltz striker Richard Gregory from Walsall Wood. Yeltz released fan favourite Gregory at the end of last season, as it seemed like he was surplus to requirements. We then had issues up front. And now Greggs has ended up with the league leaders.

But the story of ex-Yeltz forward Jack Holmes is even more interesting, especially given his relative youthfulness compared to Gregory. With Greggs being 35, you could understand the club letting him go if we thought we had better options coming in. But Holmes is 22. Another player liked by the fans, either a winger or a No 10. He's powerful, with a gift for turning and running at the opposition and causing problems. He's hard working too. To my mind he only seemed to have one major development point in his game - he needs to release the ball, or get his shot off, quicker. That seemed easily solvable.

Despite being a regular under previous manager Paul Smith, Holmes' minutes were limited under Russ Penn. Holmes left for Stamford at the end of last season - whose decision that was, we do not know. Stamford then played EFL League 1 side Rotherham in a pre-season friendly. They liked the look of Holmes and offered him a professional contract. Of course, I have no idea what went on behind closed doors with Holmes and Penn. Holmes might have left on his own accord, or Penn might have had a good reason to not retain him. But if Jack ends up with a full-time footballing career out of it, then fate acted for the best.

October

Saturday 5 October 2024, Redditch United FC Vs Halesowen Town FC - FA Trophy 3rd round qualifier

This week Roberto, proprietor of Roberto's Bar in the town, issued a dire warning. He said that if things do not change, by the end of the decade there will be no pubs left in the country. He said it's currently extremely hard to turn a profit as a publican. This did not help lift mood going into this Redditch game, as I was not really looking forward to going there for the 3rd time this season. Especially with their plastic pitch and cold burgers.

To avert the need for a burger, or anything else from the catering, I took the precaution of taking a Tesco sandwich. I originally chose prawn but then hastily switched to cheese and pickle, so I could not be accused of being part of what Roy Keane famously called the 'prawn sandwich brigade.' What Keane meant by this phrase was people who go to football matches but are not traditional fans, instead using luxury facilities, such as hospitality boxes.

At the Valley Stadium at Redditch, you can have a slice of the 'prawn sandwich brigade' experience. Their lovely first-floor lounge bar has a wonderful view over the pitch, so if you watch the game from there it's rather like being in a hospitality box. For me, I much rather prefer to be outside in the fresh air on the terraces, especially after being cooped up working in my office all week.

I always think of the FA trophy as being our version of the League Cup, a secondary chance of Wembley glory, in addition to the FA Cup. But contradictorily it's more like our version of the FA Cup. Because to get to Wembley, we still must negotiate one qualifying round and 7 rounds proper.

In an amazing run in 2019–20, knocking out 3 National League sides, we made it to the semi-finals. We eventually lost 2-1 to Concord Rangers. It was made a one-legged semi-final because of COVID, and the coin toss favoured the opposition.

But until 2019–20 we had only got to the 3rd round proper. So, making it to Wembley in May this year, or anywhere year, will be tough. But like the FA Cup, what you hope for is a good run or a good occasion - a decent team from a higher division down the Grove or an away day to their place.

One player who will not be going to Wembley, or anywhere else with the Yeltz, is Ryan Boothe. According to the Southern League's official register of players, he's no longer registered with the club. I'm assuming he felt that the introduction of Jordan Ponticelli meant that minutes and starts for him would be even more limited. Good luck to him for the future.

On Saturday's evidence, Ponticelli is definitely worth more than Ryan Boothe and Luisiana put together. But the front man was not the only new breath of fresh air. Russ Penn changed the formation to 4-4-2 and suddenly, we looked like a football team. Adventurous and cohesive going forward, with good patterns of play with the ball on the floor. And compact and organised defensively.

Wynter and Wollacott solid at the heart of the defence, ably flanked by Mitchell and Hickman at full backs, who supported and overlapped enterprising wide men Tee and Mini Macca. Smile and Parker were full of passing and endeavour in the middle of the park, and Ponticelli and Donnelly were too hot to handle up front. Platty in goal kept a clean sheet, so enough said.

For the first time this season, we built steady, concerted pressure on the opposition goal. With full backs pushing on and 2 strikers, it was too much for Redditch to cope with. Coupled with the quality of our passing and play, it was a joy to watch, and Kenny and I were enthralled.

Just after the 30-minute mark the Redditch defence could hold out no more. Their keeper failed to keep out a powerful strike by Donnelly and we were on our way, 1-0 up. 2 more goals just after half time extended the lead beyond the reach of the home side. Mini Macca scored directly from an in-swinging corner on 47 minutes. Then from 15 yards Ponticelli smashed home a loose ball in the top corner, the way good strikers do. 3-0. It could have been more. And that's the way the game ended up, the nil as pleasing as the 3, given some of the poor goals we have conceded this season.

It's not often as a football fan that you walk away from a game thoroughly and roundly pleased by your team's performance - but this was one of them. After conceding an equaliser here deep into injury time in the league, and a miserable loss in the FA Cup, this was, in the words of one of our anthems, quite simply a beautiful day.

One of the things to make it even more beautiful was a ridiculous piece of skill by Mini Macca in the first half. The ball came to him at pace above his shoulder, and what's worse he was on the touchline. With his wand-like left foot he managed to pluck the ball out of the air, and with his second and third touch, bring it down and keep it in play. And this was all under extreme pressure by a Redditch midfielder. It was truly breathtaking. Whatever the result or the performance is like, you can usually guarantee that McKauley Manning will produce at least one moment that justifies the admission fee. Today was no exception.

Credit to the manager today for changing things and trying something different. Because some managers stick to a system, or way of playing, as they are too dogmatic, stubborn, or principled. But a reluctance to change can often lead to a bad outcome for a manager, like relegation, not getting promoted, or the sack. Penn has had criticism from some sections of the support recently, so I hope he's taken some satisfaction from today.

Kenny and I walked away from the Valley stadium towards the car in the warm autumn sunshine, in the glow of victory, looking forward to our evening ahead. Who should run past us, at a full sprint, towards his car, but ex-Yeltz favourite Nathan Hayward. He'd been at the game today to cheer on the Yeltz, because his current team Worcester City had no fixture.

As I shuffled along on my walking stick, Hayward's youthful dash made me feel very old. It made me momentarily dwell on if I will ever realise my dream of seeing the Yeltz in the National League proper. Given the result and the performance we had just witnessed, I put the melancholy thought to the back of my mind with the speed of Hayward's sprint.

Monday 7 October 2024. FA Trophy 1st round proper draw

We've been drawn at home against Congleton Town, who play in the Northern Premier League West division, at step 4. So, effectively a level below us. The game is on Saturday 26 October, which currently leaves Kenny and I with a dilemma. Villa are at home to Bournemouth on the same day at 3pm. Let's hope Sky Sports or TNT do the honourable thing, and move the Villa game to a more convenient kick off time.

I messaged Holly Bush Dave to tell him who we had drawn. Dave has this thing about trying to visit as many Wetherspoons pubs as he can. He messaged back, "I've done Congleton Spoons." I replied, "That sounds like a Morris dance."

Today Yeltz TV published the gaffer's post-match Redditch interview on YouTube. An upbeat Russ Penn signed off with the titillating line that there will be more good news in the week. I'm guessing this means we are signing another new player. But could it mean that the East Terrace is getting a roof? Or that the club have bought legendary club fan and official Mankini Dave a fleece lined mankini for the winter? Who knows. We'll just have to wait and see.

Saturday 12 October 2024, Kidderminster Harriers FC Vs Guiseley Association Football Club - FA Cup 4th qualifying round

The 'more good news in the week' that Russ Penn spoke of was finally announced on Wednesday – the club is selling a Christmas range of gifts that includes Yeltz Speedos-style swimming trunks.

But it turned out on Thursday that the Speedos were only a starter. The main course is that the club have signed 27-year-old Musa Ceesay Ceesay from Redditch to bolster midfield options. Ok, go on then, I'll say it - so good they named him twice.

Musa played for C F Sant Jaume de llierca in Catalonia, Lye Town, and Wolverhampton Casuals before joining Redditch in 2023. Going from fine wine and olives in tavernas in Catalonia, to scratchings and real ale in earthy pubs in the Black Country, must have been quite a culture shock for him. But hopefully he's settled in by now.

It is international weekend, so with no distraction of an Aston Villa match I feel a bit cheated that there is no Yeltz game. With us being knocked out of the FA Cup, our league fixture against Lowestoft has been postponed, as they are still in it.

But the silver lining to this cloud is that it gave me the opportunity to visit Aggborough for the first time this season to see my mistress, in the form of Kidderminster Harriers FC. They faced Guiseley AFC, of the Northern Premier League Premier Division, a step below them. I am fond of Kiddy and like to get to Aggborough when I can. If the Yeltz and Villa are my polygamous wives, Kiddy are my bit on the side.

I was going unaccompanied, as Kenny was on a social with his Sunday football team. Which does not bother me, as I'm happy to be undistracted and immerse myself in a game of football. But at the eleventh hour my mate Jim decided to come, a pleasant change as I had not seen him in a while.

Aggborough is over 10 miles away, across mostly countryside. So, it's a marvel that there's a bus service that departs from by my house and drops you a short walk from the stadium. And for just £2. Or in the case of this trip, for free.

As Jim and I went to pay, the driver said, "Just get on." Confused, I said, "But I've not paid." The driver simply said in a louder voice, bordering on a shout, "JUST GET ON!" I was guessing he meant the device that took electronic payments was not working, so do not worry about paying. But he either did not have the communication skills, or the inclination, to say this.

At journey's end, the driver did another bizarre thing. As we were coming towards our stop, I pressed the red button, to indicate to the driver that we wanted to alight. But instead of driving to the stop, he put the brakes on, stopping the bus there and then and opened the doors. The bus stop was about 200 yards down the road. But I did not dare to ask that he drive on to it, as he did not look in the mood for taking the request well. Besides, it was sunny day, and the extra walk was welcome.

What was not welcome was the standard of football by Kiddy, who to summarise, were pretty awful. After Ashley Hemmings failed to score a penalty on the half hour, Kiddy did not convert their pressure into a goal. They were then sucker-punched by the visitors with 5 minutes to go with their only proper attack of the second half to that point. 0-1 to Guiseley was the final score.

In the second half the sun increasingly faded, and the cold crept in. It left us longing for the welcoming arms of the King & Castle, the fine pub at Kidderminster Severn Valley Railway station. We soon arrived there after the final whistle, with me rejoicing about how much I love a pub on a railway station. The Railwayman's Arms at Bridgnorth, and the Great Western in Wolverhampton, are other favourites of mine. But in no time, the last bus just after 6 saw us hurtling towards Roberto's Bar in Halesowen.

I planned to go from Roberto's Bar to Halesowen Cycling and Athletic Club. There was a middle-aged punk band double-header on, featuring the Dogs with two Dicks and Council Pop. But I did not factor in one critical element - when a man with Glaswegian roots is sitting on a bar stool in a hostelry that he likes, and he's in the mood for drinking, there is no moving him. And that was the case with Jim. I did not protest too much. But the consequences were predictable. At least by the end of the night, unlike Kiddy boss Phil Brown I'd imagine, I'd forgotten about the dire game I had seen a few hours earlier.

Saturday 19 October 2024, Bishop Stortford FC Vs Halesowen Town FC - Southern League Premier Central

This promised to be a tricky game. It turned out to be a 4 ½ hour journey for the Yeltzfolk to Woodside Park, against the side who were in the National League North only last season. Before kick-off there were only 3 points between the sides, with the home side having a game in hand. Yeltz sat in 10th but only 2 points off the play-off places, and in a mood of general optimism after the resounding win, and successful tactical switch, at Redditch.

I felt disappointed I was not going, but Kenny and I were taking in Fulham v Villa. So, we eagerly followed updates from the Yeltz game on X. The first one was heartening – I was delighted to see that Russ Penn had stuck with the 4-4-2 formation that worked so well in the last game. And an unchanged line up, except one odd change – new midfield signing Musa Ceesay replaced Todd Parker. Odd because Parker played well at Redditch, and having won 3-0, you would think Penn would simply go with the same team. But maybe Parker was not 100% fit, or Penn favoured Ceesay's extra physicality.

I immersed myself in the proceedings at Craven Cottage, so I only checked my phone at half-time. The news from Woodside Park was good – Yeltz were 1-0 up by means of a Donnelly goal on 18 minutes, and according to the updates, were dominant.

With Villa being 3-1 up deep into 7 minutes of injury time, I could not help but look at X to see how Yeltz were faring. Normally, I would do this with a great deal of anxiety. But today, for once, with the new 4-4-2 formation, and the addition of Ponticelli up front, I had a quiet confidence.

We were winning 2-1, with Keiren Donnelly having scored to retake the lead on 88 minutes, after Bishop Stortford equalised just before the hour. But it was not full time - it was 90+5. Which meant a frantic few moments of refreshing my phone, until two of the most beautiful words you can get on social media popped up – 'full-time.'

KD's 2 goals takes him up to 9 for the season. Not a bad return for a player who was effectively thrown into the forward position out of necessity because of lack of options. KD is a fan's favourite for good reason – he's a true lionheart who will put every ounce of effort into every game and will not give defenders a minute's peace. That coupled with his pace and talent, makes him a real asset.

This is a significant result. Not only in terms of the league position - 7th, a point behind the play-off's spots. But hopefully it will mean that the manager will now continue with the 4-4-2 system, which could reap rewards for us. A defeat today, and he could have deemed the system change as a failed experiment. Then reverted to 3 at the back, which produced inconsistent results, and mainly unattractive football.

In his post-match interview on Yeltz TV the manager looked pleased, and rightly so. Sometimes it seems clear that systems or signings need a refresh. But it's amazing how many managers stubbornly retain faith in them. It looks like Russ Penn has not only had the wisdom to deviate from the 3 at the back system, but also to concede that Adi Yussuf has not been the success everyone had hoped for. And well done to the board for backing the gaffer in bringing in Jordan Ponticelli.

Beyond bringing in any squad players for support, it finally feels like the jigsaw is complete. And the best jigsaws are the ones that take a while to put together.

Saturday 26 October 2024, Halesowen Town FC Vs Congleton Town FC - FA Trophy 1st round proper

When I was a 10-year-old boy and Villa won the league title in 1981 - and the European Cup the year after - the football they played somehow seemed attainable, something to aspire to. Like most boys, I dreamed of being a professional footballer. I was captain of my school football team and represented the district, and sometimes the county. When I watched Villa, being a professional player seemed somehow in reach.

Even though the players were incredibly talented, the game then seemed somehow simpler. Most teams played 4-4-2, patterns of play were easier to understand, the ball moved from back to front quicker, and it was more physical. Wingers either crossed the ball or took on their man. Defenders defended. When you had the ball midfielders attacked, and when you did not, they defended. Strikers were not expected to track back. Goalkeepers sole function was to keep the ball out of the net.

The gap between an aspiring, talented, schoolboy footballer and the higher reaches of the professional game did not seem so great - even if realistically it was, because I ended up playing all my football in the middling reaches of non-League.

By contrast, the football that Villa played in the Champions League on Tuesday night at Villa Park against Bologna, was football from another planet. Intricate movement, slide rule passing - even from the goalkeeper, Emi Martinez, under impossible pressure in his own 6-yard box – and scintillating moves. The high line defending would give centre halves Ken McNaught and Allan Evans, from the 80's team, heart murmurs. Villa won 2-0.

It's space age football, played by footballers so fit and well-conditioned that they are almost like robots. Anathema to their steak-eating, beer-drinking counterparts from the 80s. There's no doubt that Unai Emery has performed wonders with Aston Villa, and like the great 80's team, they are entertaining to watch. The game now at the top level is played with incredible high skill and technique. To such an extent that if my 10-year-old self was watching, my dream of being a professional footballer would quickly fade.

So, after the star-studied stellar mid-week football, I was looking forward to getting back to the earthiness of the Grove today. Although Villa were at home to Bournemouth, I plumped for the glamour of the FA trophy, dreaming of Wembley and the merry month of May.

Congleton Town FC, of the Northern Premier League Division One West division - one step below us - stood in our way. One quirk of their league stats prior to the game was that they had both scored and conceded 23. So, I was hoping for an open game.

At times the Grove feels like one of coldest football grounds in England. The Hawthorns, home of West Bromwich Albion FC, is the highest ground above sea level in all the top 92 clubs in England. The Grove is not too far away. On a cold winter day, the biting wind seems to whip in all the way from the Urals, with nothing to stop it.

But today beautiful autumnal sunshine engulfed the ground. It was so temperate my coat was a mere accessory slung over my shoulder, and my Yeltz scarf was only needed to mark my tribe, and not for warmth.

Regardless of the temperature, I always have a warm feeling inside Grove, as it feels like home and the people are like family. On the way in I joked with turnstile operator Nick, and buying something in the club shop was not just a plain transaction but a friendly chat with Debbie behind the counter. And then there's the friends, acquaintances, and characters I know, and talk to, on match day.

My mate Jim followed up his recent outing to Aggborough with his first visit to the Grove this season. But my excitement at revealing the new electronic scoreboard to him was dashed, as I quickly spotted that it was not working.

The other thing I quickly spotted was the size and presence of new midfielder Musa Ceesay. As he warmed up on the immaculate turf it was hard to miss him. He stood the tallest player on the pitch, and pound for pound probably one of the heaviest too. But all athletic muscle, offering us strength in the middle, which will become particularly useful when the pitches become heavier.

As the early stages of the game developed, four things became clear: Congleton have the best kit I've seen this season – yellow V-neck jerseys, with a black sash; the referee was young, but very good, and will probably make his way up through the leagues; the Yeltz were not quite at it; and, Congleton were no mugs.

The open game that I'd been hoping for was being enacted before us, and there were plentiful chances for both teams. But a combination of poor finishing and good goalkeeping kept the score at 0-0 at the break. You'd have to say that with Congleton being the lower ranked team, they were winning on points. Russ Penn had work to do at half time.

And whatever Penn said at the break did the trick. To such an extent, that in a 5-minute spell between 50 and 55 minutes, I could not text Yeltz goal updates to Kenny at Villa Park quick enough. By then we were 3-0 up, the opener a close-range finish from Tee, followed quickly by Ceesay's first goal for the club - a 25-yard strike that was deflected into the net.

The best in that frantic goal burst was the 3rd, scored by the magic man himself, Mini Macca. He picked the ball up on the edge of the box and was quickly surrounded by a clutch of opposition defenders. But like the Artful Dodger, he bobbed and weaved passed 3 or 4 of them, leaving them spellbound, before dispatching ball into bottom corner of the goal. Undiluted brilliance.   My favourite moment of the season so far, leaving me in a state of pure delirium.

Later Manning conjured another moment of breathtaking artistry. He was facing up the left- back, wide, just outside the box. Macca was right in front of the defender, with the ball at his feet, at a standstill. But at this stage of the game, even though Macca had tempted the full-back with the sight of the ball, the defender had the good sense not to take the bait. He knew the fleet footed winger would dance around him.

But even though there was no space between the two men, and it seemed impossible, with the blink of an eye, quicksilver movement, and masterful control, Manning beat him. The hapless full-back took his legs, to the sound of the fans in the Shed End shouting in unison, "PENALTY!!!" The referee deemed the foul to be outside the box and gave a free kick. Even though what we had just seen was more than deserving of a spot kick, in some ways it did not matter. Just to witness it was a privilege, and a thing of great joy and beauty. For us fans that is, not for the full-back.

Our habit of conceding off corners saw Chadwick head in for Congleton on the hour, to give them a flicker of hope. But as the sun slowly fell lower over the Harry Rudge stand so did the spirits of the Congleton players. Finally, Ponticelli put the tie to bed. He converted a penalty deep into stoppage time, after the hard-working Donnelly was tripped in the box, to make it 4-1.

With the new electronic scoreboard out of action, one thing that is working is the new 4-4-2 system. Since the manager made the change, we have won 3 in a row. Penn acknowledged this in his post-match interview on Yeltz TV saying, "At the moment it's going well, and we have found a structure and the players to fit that structure."

Spalding, who are 5 points behind us in the league, travel to the Grove on Saturday. But prior to that is the excitement of seeing what the FA Trophy draw throws up on Monday. But for now, it's off to Roberto's Bar to taste the best beer possible - winning beer.

Monday 28 October 2024. FA Trophy 2nd round proper draw

There were two significant knowns prior to this draw. Firstly, we could not draw Stourbridge, as they were knocked out of the Trophy by Alvechurch on Saturday. And secondly, there would be no Aston Villa fixture clash to worry about on the date of the 2nd round proper, as another round of international games are scheduled.

The significant unknown, of course, is who we will play, and where. When those two blanks were filled, the news could not have been more spectacular. It prompted an excited shout of, "F*CKING GET IN THERE!!!", followed by numerous fist pumps and high pitched "hee, hee, hee!!!"s at just after 1pm from my home office, that left Lisa thinking I'd won the lottery -

which, in footballing terms, I had. Because after drawing Redditch away in both the FA Cup and a previous round of the Trophy, the footballing gods had now atoned with an irresistible draw – Kidderminster Harriers away.

It is not only a brilliant local derby, but the additional spin is that it's Russ Penn's former club as manager and player. It will be a tough one, with them being in the National League North - one division above us. But it is winnable.

Then the thing happened that always occurs when I'm this excited about an event - panic kicked in. My thoughts quickly spiralled out of control, with such ludicrous things as, "What if I cannot get a ticket?", "What if I fall ill and cannot go to the game?", "What if I die before the game is played?!!!" The latter would be particularly galling, as I would not even be able to listen to the live commentary or watch the highlights. But after a few minutes of this irrational turmoil, I managed to bring myself back to calm, and reality.

It's funny to think that this season I have witnessed Villa beat Bayern Munich at Villa Park, in their first return to Europe's elite competition in more than 40 years. And yet this FA Trophy game at Kidderminster will be by far the biggest game of my season so far. It's all relative, as they say.

November

Saturday 2 November 2024, Halesowen Town FC Vs Spalding United FC - Southern League Premier Central

The sad folding of Walsall Wood FC, of the Northern Premier League Division One Midlands, has led to Yeltz signing 25-year-old midfielder Nick Clayton-Phillips. It's another reason to be confident ahead of this clash against a Spalding side who sit 5 points below us in the table, just above the relegation places.

Clayton-Phillips is a Halesowen lad, so hopefully he's found his home. He started out at West Bromwich Albion, before moving on to Braintree Town, Solihull Moors, and Kidderminster Harriers. My first impression from photographs is that he looks a lot like Yeltz player Todd Parker. With them both playing in midfield, this could be a problem for me. Especially with my habit of getting players mixed up. Mind you, I'm a lot better since I succumbed to wearing glasses.

Before the glasses, the final straw came at Villa Park when I mistook John McGinn for Tyrone Mings, two players very dissimilar in build, appearance, and skin colour. Kenny despaired, "C'mon Dad, you'll have to go to Specsavers." I did, and being able to see the players clearly has massively enhanced the enjoyment of watching football. Mind you, there have been a few games since where it would have been wiser to not wear glasses.

Talking of glasses, you could ask Yeltz fans if they are in glass half full or half empty mood. We were 9th in the table before kick-off, and before the start of the season many would have hoped for better moving into November. But we are only a point behind the play-offs, and 6 behind the leaders, on the back of 3 wins, following the successful system change. My glass was half full. Though only metaphorically speaking of course, because you are only allowed plastic glasses on the terraces at the Grove.

I got to the ground early because the club shop was selling special Yeltz poppy pin badges for Remembrance Day, with the money going to charity. Naturally, I wanted one. But I was crushed to find out that they had already sold out - from a young sales assistant wearing a Yeltz poppy pin badge.

Defeated, I walked slowly to the catering hut to get a consoling burger. To be served by a chirpy woman also donning a Yeltz poppy pin badge. In fact, to my dismay, as I walked to my spot on the East Terrace everywhere my eyes landed, someone was wearing a pin badge. It's amazing how such a small thing can lead to such big jealousy. The lesson here is to get to the ground earlier next year to buy one – lest I forget.

Kenny and I were pleased to be joined for this game by an old friend, Phil the Dray. As his team, West Bromwich Albion, had played the night before, he wisely took the opportunity of joining us at the Grove.

There was a keen sense of anticipation around the ground that come 5 o'clock we'd have 3 more points. That anticipation was met by the players with a rousing start to the game. It culminated in a penalty on 10 minutes. Mini Macca went clean through, and keeper

Breedon took his legs. But after cooly slotting his spot-kick into the corner last week, Ponticelli chose to go down the middle, and Breedon saved it.

The save lifted Spalding, and 2 minutes later the game turned on its head. They took the lead through Tomlinson, after poor Yeltz defending. Yeltz had the better of the rest of first half with a lot of possession and pressure. But we could not force the equaliser, despite a couple of chances.

A blow came just before the break when Mini Macca injured himself winning a thunderous 50-50 challenge. We love Mini Macca primarily for his sublime skills and technique. But he is not shy in the tackle, he has a good work rate, and he has an incredible leap, meaning for a smaller player he's incredibly good in the air.

Macca did not respond sufficiently to treatment at the break, so early in the second half was replaced by debutant Nick Clayton-Phillips. It quickly became clear that Clayton-Phillips is an impressive talent, with good close control, movement, and a desire to get on the ball.

With Clayton-Phillips' and Tee's invention, Parker and Smiles' impressive ball retention in midfield, and Mitchell and Cassidy raiding forward from full-back, pressure mounted on Spalding. But the visitors defended well, and we could not seem to craft a clear-cut chance. But it turned out we did not need one. Because on 77 minutes Ponticelli decided it was time to atone for his penalty miss. He picked up the ball 20 yards out, and arrowed it across goal into the bottom corner, leaving keeper Breedon with no chance. A stunning strike, 1-1.

With a quarter of the game left it felt like a matter of time before we forced the winner - but it would not come. Countless crosses went into the box, with nobody on the end of them. And top scorer KD was just having one of those games where nothing was going for him, despite all his efforts. Credit to Spalding, they defended well.

As the 6 minutes of stoppage time slipped away, it looked like it was going to end 1-1. I was getting myself ready to feel philosophical about the draw. Sometimes in these moments you need a cool head and a touch of class, and it came in the form of experienced midfielder Josh Smile. He picked the ball up 25 yards out, to the right of the box, and controlled it. Instead of simply lumping it into the mixer, he looked up and spotted Donnelly and expertly chipped the ball into him. With his back to goal and closely marked, KD ushered the ball on his chest to his left, swivelled, and from 12 yards out sweetly shot across the keeper with his right foot into the bottom corner.

Mayhem. I was lost in ecstasy. The Shed erupted, the Spalding players out on their feet. There are different types of wins in football, and they are all good. But the last-minute winner, especially of such quality as KD's strike, is simply the best.

Thankfully, the final whistle followed soon after without us having to endure too many nervy moments. It marked a 2-1 win to the Yeltz, and 4 victories on the spin. Over his football watching decades Phil has been to countless grounds over the length and breadth of the country, to watch Albion and other teams. Because he just loves football. But he would not have seen many more dramatic climaxes than this one.

Left-back Reece Mitchell was voted man of the match by the sponsors, and I'm delighted for him. Mitch must be a manager's delight, because he's utterly dependable and never seems to have a bad game. His positioning and decision-making are always spot on, he can defend one-on-one, and he's an asset going forward too. I'm chuffed for him that now we're playing 4-4-2, as he's become an important part of the team once more.

Other than leaving us in a state of unmitigated joy, the win leaves us 8th in the table. But we are only 3 points behind leaders Kettering. They also had a joyful weekend, winning at their local rivals Northampton Town, from EFL League 1, in the FA Cup 1st round proper. Stourbridge sit one place above us, but we are level on points with a game in hand. We've also played one less game than most the teams above us.

We play our game in hand on Tuesday at Lowestoft, which will be tough. It's a long journey for a midweeker, and they will be rested after having had no fixture today. But as Russ Penn said in his post-match interview on Yeltz TV, "We've got to keep the standards because if we do, we will be a match for anyone." Too right gaffer – onwards and upwards.

Tuesday 5 November 2024, Lowestoft Town FC Vs Halesowen Town FC - Southern League Premier Central

Realistically, this 10 hour round trip was off the agenda for me. It would involve an afternoon off work for a 2 o'clock coach and arriving back at Halesowen in the middle of the night. Fatigue is the main side effect of the medication I take for the neurological condition I live with. So, this trip would have wiped me out for the rest of the week. But I admire the supporters who go on these far-flung mid-week journeys. They are the heart and soul of the club and deserve immense credit.

After a poor start to the season, newly promoted Lowestoft have settled, and had not lost in the last 4 games. Before kick-off there was only 4 points between them and us. There have been nearly 4 goals on average in Lowestoft's league games this season, and 16 in the Yeltz's last 5 league outings. So, this game promised plenty of fireworks, which would be fitting, given that it's bonfire night.

A footnote on Lowestoft Town is that Ipswich Town, Glasgow Rangers, and England great Terry Butcher is president of the club. He spent his early years growing up in the town.

Before this game, my rising sense of anxiety over tickets for the Kidderminster Harriers FA Trophy fixture finally ended. As there was no news on tickets, and the date edged increasingly closer, my nerves grew corresponding worse. I just wanted a ticket in my hand to secure my right of entry.

I got so desperate, I sent an enquiring email to committee member Paul Essom at the Yeltz. To my relief, the ever-helpful Paul quickly replied to say Harriers are making tickets available on their website on that day. Tickets purchased, now I only have to fret about tickets for the derby at bitter rivals Stourbridge on 30 November.

I put on Halesowen Town Radio for live match commentary. It reminded me of hearing the voice of someone like Peter Jones in the 1970's on BBC radio, for a midweek European night on a crackly line. Although Lowestoft is not as far away as Belgrade or Frankfurt, in relative terms it feels like it. The east coast of Suffolk on a Tuesday night is another world, and I felt excited and privileged that it was being broadcast into my living room.

As the game started it was clear that the Yeltz were up for it. This was related by young commentator Tom Cartwright, under the guiding wing of experienced co-commentator Frank Williams. Usual lead commentator Matt Ponter, who would not be out of place on *Match of the Day*, could not escape work for the biblical trip. It's delightful that Tom has quickly grown in confidence and delivery in his craft, and his enthusiasm carried the broadcast.

About 50 odd Yeltz faithful made the mammoth trip. But they were creating noise far beyond their number, singing their full repertoire including: "Oh, Halesowen is wonderful, oh, Halesowen is wonderful, we've got a Spoons and an Asda, oh, Halesowen is wonderful!"

I love the fact that on non-League radio broadcasts that you can clearly hear the full colour of the crowd's musings. On this broadcast you could hear things like, "That number 3 is sh*t!" and "That was a foul, you f*cking prick!" Unlike on national radio channels, the commentators rarely apologise for unsavoury language, otherwise they would have little time to describe the game.

Touchingly the Yeltz fans also sung, "There's only one Keith McKenna", in reference to our chairman, who together with the rest of the board, has done fantastic work for the club. It's not often a crowd sing favourably about the Chair, so it is quite an accolade. But one well deserved, as in recent history the club was in quite a mess under previous ownership. So, we all deeply appreciate the work of our dedicated board, staff, and volunteers.

The fireworks that were promised before the game did not take too long to go off. And driven on by the noisy Yeltzers, it came in the form our very own firecracker. KD capitalised on a mistake after 10 minutes to open the scoring. KD's strike partner Ponticelli extended the lead to 2-0 on 38 minutes, after a good decision by the referee to play on. It felt like it was going to be our night.

This was confirmed after the break, because despite the dry weather, it was raining goals. Strikes on 65 from Conor Tee, and two more from red hot KD on 69 and 76, lead to a 5-0 win. The hat-trick catapulted KD to become the league's leading scorer with 10 goals, 13 overall for the season. He has also become the first Yeltz player to score in 5 consecutive league matches since another fan's favourite, Ben Haseley, in 2013/14.

By full-time I was in second heaven, because the win pushed up to second in the league. We are equal on points with top team Kettering, but they have a superior goal difference and a game in hand.

If ever a performance deserved the label 'statement win', this was it. A long midweek trip, against an in-form opposition, on what was apparently a testing pitch. And we thrashed them. It is not like me to be so bold, but what the hell, I'm getting carried away with the moment - Kettering, we are coming for you.

Saturday 9 November 2024, Halesowen Town FC Vs AFC Sudbury - Southern League Premier Central

I did not know whether to feel emboldened by my uncharacteristic, 'Kettering, we are coming for you!' rallying cry from Tuesday, or regretful of it, ahead of this game. Often a red face can follow such a bold statement.

If I were Russ Penn, having won 5 on the bounce and having scored 16 goals, I'd be endeavouring to keep everyone grounded. And I'm sure he is. As a player and a coach my mantra was the clichéd 'one game at a time.' And though I am a fan now, and I am allowed to get excited, I have not much changed.

When we were going through a poor spell, I encouraged gloomy Yeltzfolk to keep the faith, because I felt we were close to improvement. And now we are winning, we need to keep level heads. It's a very competitive division and a long season. For starters, we have 11 more games in just over 7 weeks before the turn of the year. For now, we are going great guns, but we need to keep the focus.

Before kick-off Sudbury were 10th in the league, 6 points behind us, and that told me two things. Firstly, if we play our best, and take our chances, we'll win. But, secondly, and importantly, any team sitting in mid-table in this division are a tough prospect, and not to be underestimated.

A quick factoid about the opposition is that the 'A' in AFC Sudbury does not stand for association, amateur, or athletic. It stands for 'amalgamated.' The club was formed in 1999 by the merger of Sudbury Town and Sudbury Wanderers. In their short history they have won the Eastern Counties League Premier division 5 seasons on the trot, and reached the FA Vase final 3 consecutive times, both being records.

I always keep a keen eye on the weather prior to the game, usually using the Met Office's app, as I tend to find it the most accurate. On this occasion the TV was on, and the BBC's weatherman was saving me the trouble. But he was proving to be rather irritable, because not only was he telling us the forecast but also his views on in.

For days it has been dry, overcast, not windy, and quite temperate for the time of year - pretty good if you ask me, and co-incidentally, perfect weather for football. But the weatherman said this spell of 'miserable' weather was coming to an end, and we might see the sun to cheer us up. What would cheer me up is if weather broadcasters stuck to their jobs and kept their opinions to themselves.

One person's miserable weather is another's heaven, and I fall into the latter category, not being a summer type. We do not want the sun dazzling Platty as he's about to catch the ball, after all.

Kenny and I were joined at an expectant Grove by two Tony's – Abbo and Dot. The former friend makes it to several Yeltz games a season. But the latter lives in Warwick now and has a young child, so was delighted to be watching football for a change, instead of CBeebies. Dot is so nicknamed as he looks like the former EastEnders character Dot Cotton. But ironically, unlike the gentle, elderly lady from the soap, on the football field he would have smashed his own grandmother if it guaranteed 3 points.

I did play football with Abbo too, but he's more renowned for his cricket talent, having taken well over 1,000 wickets in club cricket. As Chairman of Netherton CC, he also has the dubious honour of awarding himself Chairman's player of the season. Which I gather hit a few people for 6.

Because of our electric form, Yeltzfolk could not wait for this game to start. But there were more important matters to attend to first. Being the closest game to Remembrance Sunday it was important we partook in the relevant commemorations. The club did it in style, with members of the armed forces, the *Last Post*, a touching reading of *For the Fallen* by our beloved stadium announcer Paul Essom, followed by a perfectly observed 2-minute silence.

As remembrance services have always been part of our lives, it is easy to think that they have been held forever. But of course, they have not. And I reflected that when the Yeltz moved to the Grove in 1881, they could not have imagined the horrors of the two world wars to come. I then did what I always do at remembrance services at football grounds every year - I thought about how truly grateful I am to be standing next to my wonderful son, about to enjoy a game of football, as a free man in a democratic country.

I remembered my dear Grandad Charlie, and the deprivations he would have gone through fighting in the Second World War. Then, just over 30 years later in 1976, in this free country of ours, he took me, his grandson, to this very football ground, the Grove. And now 48 years on, here I am today, with my son. Thank you, Grandad, for both of those things. I'll love you from the bottom of my heart, forever.

After contemplating wars, loss, and remembrance, it would be easy to say that the outcome of this match was not that important. But I'd be lying. It mattered a hellish amount, and I desperately wanted to us to win. And the sense of keenness around the stadium hinted that most other Yeltz fans felt the same. After the 5-goal mauling of Lowestoft, a thunderous opening was predicted.

But after 10 minutes Sudbury's Joe Neal had other ideas. After loose defending by the Yeltz, he turned the ball past Platty to open the scoring. We quickly countered with multiple attacks on their goal, and intuitively it did not feel like 'one of those days' where we were not going to score. Because with Jordan Ponticelli on the pitch, goals tend to follow. Just before the half hour he pounced to equalise, leaving the visitors just about scraping through to half time with the scores level at 1-1.

After the break, the game evened out a bit, but it always felt like we were building up to a renewed assault on the Sudbury goal. But then disaster – on the hour Mini Macca collected a harsh yellow card, for a foul on the halfway line. The problem being he'd already been booked in the first half. So, a red followed, and we were down to 10 men.

But quickly, a feeling of despair turned to optimism, and all down to the manager. In these circumstances most gaffers would take off a striker, and bring on a midfielder, to replace Macca. But instead, Penn simply did.....nothing. Meaning we still played with 2 strikers and 3 midfielders, one less. Psychologically and tactically, this was a masterstroke.

Psychologically, because it said both to their players and ours, and the crowd, "We are not sitting back, we're going to try and win this." And tactically, as they played 3-5-2, our 3 midfielders and 2 full backs could cope with their 5 anyway.

This positivity buoyed on the crowd, and victory was sensed. Mathaius was going like the clappers on his drum in the Shed End, who were in full voice. The vibrancy from the crowd drove on the players. The energy and commitment they showed, to make up for being a man down, was staggering. But try as they might, the goal would not come, and legs started to tire.

But with less than 10 minutes to go, KD headed the ball wide to Ponticelli. He advanced into the box at a wide angle. KD was in a much better goal scoring position, but I expected Ponticelli to shoot, with him being a goal scorer. Credit to him though, he did not, he squared it to KD, who duly tucked it into the back of the net.

It was absolute joyous pandemonium on and off the pitch. Kenny and I were jumping around and hugging each other, and I had a vague notion that he was saying something to me. But I was delirious in my own thoughts, and I could not hear him. He was saying, "Ponticelli did brilliant!" but he finally got exasperated and said, "Dad, you are not listening, you're in a world of your own!" Which of course, I was.

I watched the highlights on Yeltz TV later. When KD's goal went in any sense of impartiality from commentators Matt Ponter, and Tom Cartwright in particular, went completely out of the window. And it's understandable. It was one of the biggest league goals we've seen at the Grove for a while.

I expected our tired 10 men to camp out on the edge of our box for the remaining minutes, to try and secure the 3 points. But other than fending off a few set pieces from the visitors, it was relatively calm. And even better was to come in the last minute of stoppage time. Sub Nick Clayton-Phillips broke in confident fashion and squared the ball to the marauding Jordan Ponticelli. The striker side footed the ball home to seal the game 3-1.

All we wanted then was the referee's whistle, but another type of intervention was needed from the man in black. A fracas developed in the dugouts, and I then saw Russ Penn incredulously rubbing his face. I was told that Sudbury manager Marc Abbott had punched our gaffer. Far from doing Penn damage, it looked like the Yeltz boss had barely flinched. The linesman saw the incident and explained it to the referee. He sent Abbott off to raucous applause from the Yeltz faithful.

The linesman then probably saved the diminutive Sudbury boss's skin with his quick-thinking. To get to the tunnel, Abbott would have to walk down the East Terrace touchline, then in front of the Shed End. All in close proximity of bloodthirsty Yeltz fans, and they were not in the mood to say to him, "Never mind old sport, no hard feelings, we'll buy you a pint in the bar later." Sensing this, the linesman started to walk Abbot directly across the pitch in the direction of the tunnel and beckoned a steward to complete the walk with him.

The unfortunate thing was that the substituted KD pushed Abbot after he struck Penn, leading to a yellow card. KD had already been booked during the game, meaning he got a red card too. This means that both KD and Mini Macca are both likely to be suspended for our FA trophy game at Kidderminster next Saturday. A game we need to be full strength for, with them being a step higher in the pyramid. But that was the only downside to an afternoon of rip-snorting entertainment, where for once, the only sucker punch we were subjected to was from the opposition manager.

Kettering above us, and Telford and Stourbridge immediately below us, all won, so there's no change in the top spots, and we remain in 2nd. But in terms of entertainment, this game was definitely top spot.

Saturday 16 November 2024, Kidderminster Harriers FC Vs Halesowen Town FC - FA Trophy 2nd round proper

When the draw for this game was made back in October, after my initial excitement, I said that panic set in. I said the panic centred around things like not being able to get a ticket or falling ill and not being able to go. Once I subsequently got a ticket, my nerves settled. But this week, as I sat in the Same Day Emergency Care Unit at hospital, I started to rue the day I penned my thoughts, thinking I had jinxed myself.

I'd been experiencing palpitations all week, but my fears about anything sinister were put to bed after reading the NHS's online information. By Wednesday they subsided, so all was fine and dandy. But by Thursday things took a turn, the palpitations were back, a little bit worse, and I felt lightheaded and faint. Because of the symptoms, the NHS's online information advised me to contact my GP practice. So, I did, and they told me to go to the local hospital ASAP.

At the hospital, the mere mention of chest discomfort and faintness, from me, a middle-aged man, led to an ECG heart scan within 45 minutes. After the scan, they ushered me into the waiting room to complete a form, leaving me with the scan results underneath the form on the clipboard. I looked at the results and took notes.

I could not, of course, understand the scan's peak and trough squiggles. But I did jot down the following: 'left ventricular hypertrophy', 'sinus rhythm abnormal', and 'mid acute. St/t'. None of which sounded very good.

The waiting room was packed, and they were even handing out free hot drinks and sandwiches. So, I took this as a sign that I was in for a long wait before seeing a doctor. So, naturally I researched my notes from the scan. My fears were confirmed, and the outcome sounded bad. My thoughts ran wild. My immediate thought was, I'm going to miss the Kidderminster game, but I tried to allow myself a glimmer of hope. Then it was things like, are they going to admit me to the ward? Will they operate? How long will I be in hospital?

Eventually I was called to see a doctor. He said the EGC did not reveal anything to worry about, and my heart is fundamentally fine for a man of my age. Relieved, but confused, I asked, 'What about left ventricular hypertrophy?' Wikipedia had informed me that it is a thickening of the wall of the heart's main pumping chamber, called the left ventricle. This thickening may increase pressure within the heart. The condition can make it harder for the heart to pump blood. Which sounds extremely serious. The doctor told me not to worry too much about that. He said it's because I have slightly increased blood pressure, but that is controlled by the medication I take.

After asking me a series of questions, the doctor then said the cause of the palpitations could be things like an overactive thyroid, an infection, or a blood clot in the lung. So, they need to test for these things. An overactive thyroid? I assured him they can rule that out straight away, because being middle-aged, nothing physical about me is overactive. The doctor did not laugh. A series of blood tests and scans followed which culminated in a gruelling 8 hour stay at the hospital.

I had long waits in between each test or scan. To entertain myself I had two choices: to read, or to listen to podcasts on my headphones. But both were problematic. The podcasts, because medical staff are continually coming into the room calling out people's names, so you must listen out for yours. And besides there was a TV in the room, and repeats of Coronation Street seemed to be on a loop. So, the podcast was having to compete with the loud voices of Jack and Vera Duckworth.

Reading was also an issue. Problem being, when my name is called, I must swap my reading glasses for my normal glasses. And the clinicians do not wait. They are in such a hurry they are off down the corridor, and I did not want to miss them.

The other poser was the whole Russian roulette of when to go to the toilet. Because you know when you go, the clinician will come into the waiting room and call your name. Which is exactly what happened. I could hear my name when I was in full flow in the toilet, so I had to nip things in the bud, so to speak, halfway through. Which is harder than it sounds.

By 8.15pm they were still unsure what my issue was, but said there is a slight chance it could be a blood clot in the lung. To test for this, they need to do a CT scan, but they cannot do this until Wednesday. Until then, I need to inject myself daily with a blood thinner and avoid anything that might increase my heart rate too much, like exercise, work stress – or getting over-excited at football matches, maybe?

If I was being very sensible, I would not go to the Kidderminster game. But realistically, that was never going to happen. So, I decided, I'd go but I would have to defy human nature and try to stay calm. I did take a semi-sensible approach though and swapped mine and Newty's standing tickets for seating. I thought that I'd be calmer sitting down with the more mature Yeltz fans. Newty was happy enough, as like me he has creaky knees from too much football in his younger years.

There was a jubilant and noisy scene inside Aggborough, with an incredible 1,442 Yeltz fans in full voice, driven on by Mathaius the drummer. KD and Mini Macca were suspended, and Nick Clayton-Phillips was cup tied. So, the gaffer shrewdly decided to go with an extra midfielder, bringing in Ceesay, leaving Ponticelli up front on his own.

Kidderminster's manager Phil Brown employed a bit of kidology, because in his pre-match interview he strongly hinted that he would rest a few first team players. But he did far from that, and pretty much picked his strongest 11.

The game could not have started better for us, and on 10 minutes my pledge to not get over-excited went completely out of the window. Kiddy right-back Joe Foulkes short changed keeper Dibble with a back pass, and after Todd Parker tackled him, the ball landed at the feet of exactly the right person – Jordan Ponticelli. Having scored 6 goals in 6 games since joining the club, he was simply going to score - and he did, slotting the ball assuredly into the corner. 1-0 to the Yeltz.

Calm I was not. And neither were the other 1,441 delirious Yeltzfolk. A concerned Newty told me to compose myself, fearing I'd drop dead on the spot. Which would put a dampener on our post-match drink.

The rest of the first half was scrappy, and we withheld Kiddy pressure well. We were hoping to get to half-time a goal to the good. But that hope ended 10 minutes before the break when Reece Devine levelled the scores, after some good work by Caleb Richards down the left. 1-1.

But then just before the 45 minutes were up, Jak Hickman played a stunning ball for Ponticelli to run on to. The striker beat keeper Dibble the with his shot across goal, and for all the world it looked like we were going 2-1 up. But the ball agonisingly hit the inside of the post and bounced out.

It's fair to say that the home side had the better of a play in the second half, and we defended valiantly, led by our magnificent skipper Ryan Wynter. But we did have counterattack and set piece chances, and the clock wound down. Eventually the board went up, showing 4 minutes of stoppage time.

In the FA Trophy there is no extra time, so games go straight to penalties. I even said to Newty that Platty is a better on the line keeper than Christian Dibble, and I think he will save at least one penalty. But I'm an experienced enough football man to have not indulged in such thoughts while the game was still in progress. Because in the 92nd minute Kiddy sub Kobe Hall scored the winner, his first for the club, to break Yeltz's hearts. It finished 2-1 to Kiddy.

It was a body blow for the fans, the players, who had given absolutely everything, and the staff. And Russ Penn, on his return to Kidderminster Harriers, the club he played for 170 times, and as a manager got promoted to the National League.

But despite my bitter disappointment I was quite quickly philosophical about the result. The team and the fans had given us many reasons to be proud. And a couple of days ago I thought my ticker was knackered, so I was grateful just to go to the game.

As I stood close to the pitch giving the Yeltz players and staff the hearty round of applause they richly deserved, I reflected on what a great occasion it was for West Midlands football. Out of the 3,884 attendance 1,442 were Yeltz fans. With no Premier League or Championship games today, it was the biggest away support in the whole of England. Better than any EFL League One, League Two or National League team. Not bad for a side from the Southern League Premier Central. So, despite the defeat this is one that will live long in the memory.

Saturday 23 November 2024, Halesowen Town FC Vs Biggleswade Town FC - Southern League Premier Central

I've had a week of injecting myself with blood thinners. Then on Wednesday I went back to the hospital for a CT scan, to find out if I have a blood clot on my lung. Before the scan a nurse injected me with a dye, and said I might get a warm feeling all over for a few seconds, but not to worry. After the injection, the nurse asked me how I felt. "It feels like knocking back a Scotch," I enthused. "Well, you can't have another one!" she retorted. I said I'm glad she does not work at Roberto's Bar.

After a wait, and another free sandwich, the doctor reported the scan revealed no blood clot or anything else sinister. As a parting gift, they offered me a thyroid scan at my GP surgery, which I accepted, and I was dismissed. So, I was none the wiser as to what had caused the symptoms. But I am still alive, with all my vitals seemingly in a good working order, following my MOT. In footballing terms, you could compare it to winning a game, but you are not sure how you have won it.

Back on planet football, Villa are also at home today and selfishly kicking off at the same time as the Yeltz. But because of the weather, I went to Villa Park, because of the decent risk of Halesowen's game being postponed. This week we have had freezing temperatures and snow. And today storm Bertie arrived, bringing with it heavy rain and high winds, which were due to persist all day. I figured even if the

Yeltz game was played, the weather was so appalling, there was even a risk of abandonment.

The havoc wreaked by storm Bertie meant that parts of Britain are flooded, with some motorways shut, and power down. The only effect on our home is that a plant pot on the front drive blew over, which Lisa picked up. It made me feel very fortunate indeed. Not only that I do not live in a flood affected area, but also that Lisa did not send me out in the rain to pick up the plant pot.

Another reason for going to Villa was that I was still feeling a little sorry for myself after my recent health scare. So, it was good to be in the warm embrace of my family members that went to the game. And specifically with Kenny, he generally favours watching in-stadium Villa games over Yeltz's, given a choice. Unless it's a big one, like the number 9 derby but he's unlikely to get a ticket for next week's big game.

In defiance of the elements, the Yeltz game was unbelievably declared on. It is a great testament to the ground staff, and the team of enthusiastic volunteers. Hotshot striker KD returned after his one match ban, but Mini Macca still served a 2nd week's suspension. His wing spot went to Nick Clayton-Phillips.

Prior to the game, Biggleswade, from Hertfordshire, sat at the bottom of the league on 9 points, 8 from safety, and 20 behind the Yeltz. So, they needed a result, and would be fighting for their lives, and sometimes a heavy pitch can be a bit of a leveller.

But when I checked the score at half time at Villa Park, the news was good. KD had snatched one to put the Yeltz 1-0 up, which I'm sure would be a great psychological blow to the struggling visitors.

During a break in play at Villa Park, shortly into the second half, I peaked at the HTFC X feed. Biggleswade had gone down to 10 men, after Liam Andrews was dismissed. Being 1-0 up with the advantage of an extra man, it felt like it was going to be Yeltz's day. Unbeknownst to me, following the red card Biggleswade apparently showed great resolve, and grew into the game.

But all I knew was that at full-time we'd won 3-1, with further goals from Jordan Ponticelli and a penalty from Conor Tee. Obidinma Onyeagwara converted a penalty for Biggleswade with 5 minutes to go.

Donnelly has now scored 15, and Ponticelli 8 in 8 since joining the club. We remain in 2nd place in the table. We are 4 points behind Kettering, because they won again, and 5 points ahead of Stourbridge, ahead of next week's derby. In his post-match interview on Yeltz TV, Russ Penn seemed self-assured, confident, but calm. A man determined and focused on the job in hand.

The main thing today was we won. A parallel was the Hitchin game last season, that I described in the introduction to this book. A similar November day of heavy rain, playing a side at the lower end of the table, also coincidentally from Hertfordshire. That day, in a game we should have won, we lost 3-1. Today, we won 3-1. And this season, that seems to be the difference.

We have more tenacity and resilience to overcome these challenges, in addition to our squad's qualities.

After Villa's 2-2 draw with Crystal Palace, Kenny and I popped into Roberto's Bar for a restorative pint. Holly Bush Dave was in there and he'd been to the Yeltz game, so I enthusiastically asked him about it. Usually, the person tells you about the goals, and any major incidents first, and talks about the general overview of the game. But in typical eccentric fashion Dave concentrated on telling me about the game's bookings. But I would not have him any other way.

We play Telford, one place below us, on Boxing Day, and Kettering, on 4 January, both away. They are bubbling up to be mouth-watering fixtures. But before then, we have the little matter of the number 9 derby, at our bitter rivals Stourbridge, to look forward to next Saturday. I cannot wait.

Saturday 30 November 2024, Stourbridge FC Vs Halesowen Town FC - Southern League Premier Central

One of the main stories of this fixture developed before a ball was even kicked. When the Yeltz ticket allocation was finally announced, the news was very disappointing. Stourbridge said there are safety issues with their Shed End stand, the away end, and limited us to 475 tickets. Which means all of us season ticket holders got one, but there was precious few left over for anyone else, including Kenny. The club decided to put the 100 or so general sale tickets to ballot.

The issue with the stand happened because of a residential development on land behind the stand. The developers removed earth from a grass bank that supports the stand, leaving it potentially unstable. I am not sure whether this was within the scope of the planning permission, but looking at photographs of it, it seems unlikely.

Stourbridge FC are understandably very unhappy about the situation and are trying to resolve it as quickly as possible. Especially as the reduced ground capacity will cause them loss of earnings. Both Stourbridge and the Yeltz looked at solutions to maximise the attendance for this game, including agreeing to switch the fixture to the Grove. But inexplicably, they say the Southern League would not let them.

This naturally has resulted in a lot of disgruntled, ticketless, Yeltz fans. Some feel the ballot system is not fair, as it gives an opportunity for less loyal fans to get a ticket ahead of diehards. I understand their position. But equally it's tough for the club. I guess whichever way they distribute the spare tickets, they will probably have been criticised for something that was not their fault.

Social media and the unofficial Yeltz forum have been red hot with comment, opinion, theories, and conjecture. But in fairness, most of it has been sensible and balanced, with the odd exceptions. One thing is for sure, it's not HTFC's fault, and ultimately the issue with the stand is not Stourbridge FC's fault either.

In the event, Kenny did not get a ticket in the ballot. I of course felt guilty that I was going, and I dearly wish that he'd got a ticket too. But not guilty enough to give him my ticket. I could justify that on the basis that I'd supported the Yeltz many more years than him – but then I'm 33 years his senior, so that would be grossly unfair. But I have been to more Halesowen games than Kenny during this season, so that's one factor. The other is, he kind of owes me one anyway.....

During Euro 2020, my brother Warwick was going to the England Vs Denmark semi-final at Wembley with his son Charlie and had one spare ticket. He said he would love to invite Kenny and I but obviously could only cater for one of us. I did the fatherly thing, and insisted Kenny take the ticket for what would hopefully be the experience of a lifetime. And it was. Not only did England win 2-1 after extra-time, but they sat right by Frank Skinner and David Baddiel and had selfies with them. Of course, ultimately, in the final, football did not come home.

On the night the precious derby tickets were issued, I went to the Grove to pick mine up. Back at home, I obsessively checked the place where I store my tickets to make sure it was still there. Not that I was worried that Kenny was going nab it – after all he does not know where I hide my tickets. I was just paranoid about it, given its sanctity.

During the week of the game, I could think of little else. Even Champions League football at Villa Park during midweek could not distract me from thoughts of the number 9 derby. Mind you, it was a drab 0-0 draw against Juventus. At night, I even found my dreams were full of the derby.

I still had a sneaky feeling that somehow Kenny was going to get a ticket, but I did not know how. Then on Thursday the club announced that they'd secured a further 50 tickets, that would go into the ballot. I was convinced Kenny was going to get one. But alas, he did not. So, that was that. The last chance saloon had gone, and I finally had to accept that he was not coming to the game.

Then on Friday tea-time, Kenny called me. "Hi Dad, you'll never guess what's happened....." From the glee in his voice, I could tell straight away that he had secured a ticket. Someone he knew from his Sunday football team had a ticket but had subsequently got a ticket for West Brom's away game at Preston. They had decided to go to the latter game. So, he sold Kenny his Yeltz ticket at face value. Kenny was coming to the ball after all, and I was delighted for him.

We met Holly Bush Dave in Stourbridge Wetherspoons. He ordered his customary pre-game drinks of 2 pints of real ale and a refillable cup of coffee. He took full advantage of the 'refillable' part of the bargain.

Unusually, I ordered a low alcohol beer. Reason being, I had drunk a little bit too much the night before. I was home alone, because Lisa was working in Telford. I planned to have a quiet night in ahead of the big game, watching Southampton Vs Brighton on TV. But I was so excited I simply could not sit still. So, I decided to go to Roberto's Bar for a couple of pints. But the usual thing happened - you get chatting, then just as you are planning to go, another friend wanders in. And this pattern repeats itself, and before you know it, it's midnight.

The stroll from the Wetherspoons to Stourbridge FC's War Memorial ground was a pleasant one, and there were no signs of trouble both outside and inside the ground. Fans, stewards, and the police all seemed in good, friendly spirits. There were Christmas market stalls on Stourbridge High Street, but they seemed oddly out of place in the unseasonably warm weather. We hoped that come full-time, we would be in jolly, festive mood.

It seemed clear to me that Stourbridge's Shed End could have housed more Yeltz fans, despite the safety concerns. There were big gaps on the terraces. I understand that the welfare of fans is key, but it seems like the powers that be were overly cautious.

Similarly, the official capacity of the Grove is a ludicrous 3,150. When it is sold out, there are big gaps on the terraces and even the seats in the Harry Rudge stand are not full. We do not want to see crushes on the terraces like we did in the 1980's, but the capacity should be more reasonable. The Grove could house at least 4,000 fans quite comfortably, if not more.

Stourbridge have a 3-sided ground, as they share with the town's cricket club, so the sellout crowd for this one was 1,834. The downside for them is that they would probably not be able to progress to the National League with this stadium. But I guess at least they will never have an artificial pitch. I was glad it was a grass pitch when I played here in my footballing days, this being a ground I've run around on more than I have spectated at. Though my playing days are becoming an increasingly distant memory.

When we got there Kenny said, "I have one prediction for today, Dad. We will score a last-minute goal down this end." He then proceeded to merrily munch on his hot dog, while Holly Bush Dave regaled me with tales of bartering with his barber. He suggested to the barber that he should not have to pay the full fee for his haircut, because he has a bald patch. It worked, and he negotiated a discount.

The clock on Amblecote Holy Trinity Church, opposite the ground, struck 3 and the game began. Our Holy Trinity of Kieren Donnelly, Jordan Ponticelli, and Conor Tee made the early running and caused the Glassboys defence problems. Our other attacking bright spark, Mini Macca, had an early chance, lifting the ball over the bar.

But it was on form KD who struck first blood with his 16th goal of the season. He quickly pounced on a defensive mistake on the half hour, to prod the ball home from 12 yards. We retained our dominance for the rest of the first half but could not extend our lead. This was despite decent chances, which fell to Donnelly.

The second half was more even and combative. Stourbridge managed to get a better foothold in the game. But midway through the second half Donnelly hopefully closed down keeper Ollie Taylor, who was outside his box and set to clear the ball. Taylor launched his kick into KD and the ball fell to the striker, 20 yards from goal. He opted not to shoot first time but took a touch and advanced on goal. To his credit, Taylor recovered, made a good save, and kept his team in the game.

Then the game turned. On 82 minutes Glassboys skipper Joel Kettle bundled the ball in following a long throw. 1-1. Then disaster, and our old undoing – conceding off a corner. When the referee pointed to the corner flag, I could almost feel what was coming. It was a quality inswinging delivery, and a good header by Ethan McLeod. But we should have done more to defend it. 2-1 to Stourbridge. Given it was the 89th minute, defeat seemed inevitable.

As we entered injury time, Jak Hickman played a long ball to our left flank, asking a lot of Kieren Donnelly to catch it. KD has a turn of pace, but after a long game of nonstop running, it was asking a lot.

KD not only had to keep the touchline-bound ball in play, but he also had to deal with the physical attentions of a much bigger Stourbridge defender. Through sheer determination, he not only reached the ball but shrugged the defender off, then ran at him along the goal line, right in front of us. With a combination of skill, speed, and bloody-minded grit to hold off the stronger man, KD wriggled his way past the defender, on the goal line, now just inside the 18-yard box. The defender had to let him go, as any kind of challenge would have resulted in a penalty.

We looked up to see who KD could cross the ball to or pick out with a pass. As expected, Ponticelli was in a prime goal scoring position, in the middle of the sticks, and Hickman was rapidly advancing into the box. But our dynamite striker had other ideas. He hit a rapid snapshot, from a ridiculously tight angle, almost from the goal line, high in between Taylor's goalkeeper gloves. Inexplicably, it sailed into the roof of the net. I've never witnessed a better equaliser. 2-2.

The pandemonium was so great in the away end, my glasses flew off, I lost my walking stick, and I did not know who to hug first, Kenny, Dave, or both. In that beautiful moment of pure undistilled ecstasy I did not give a fiddler's fart about my glasses, my stick, or anything else. Kenny and I jumped and swayed and laughed and screamed, as loud as our lungs allowed.

Even after the joyful chaos started to settle down, there was a sense of pure disbelief of what we had just witnessed. How KD had managed to keep the ball in and beat a defender, who had a fine game, was one thing. But to score from a simply impossible angle, was another. One thing is for sure - I'll never see a goal quite like that again. It was truly as unique as it was spectacular. It was as much a testament to desire and determination, as it was to talent and ability. And that's why us Yeltzfolk love Kieren Donnelly.

The 3 blasts of the referee's whistle disappeared off into the Black Country darkness to signal honours even, with a 2-2 draw. But after snatching a point from the jaws of defeat, and with such an electrifying goal, it felt like a win.

As they always do, the Yeltz players and staff approached us buoyant fans, as we belted out a medley of favourite songs, to show their appreciation for our support. And this is not like the Premier League where they generally keep a good 30 or 40-yards distance. They come right up to the stand, many players shaking hands with fans and having selfies. They do this win, lose, or draw. This helps forge a more familial bond between fans and those wearing the badge on the field. And this aids both parties – the fans cheer and sing louder for their heroes, and the players give everything for the faithful.

A point was not so bad against a decent Glassboys side. We will meet them again at the return fixture at the Grove in February. The result means we have closed the gap on top side Kettering to 3 points, us remaining in 2nd. But they have a game in hand, as they play in the FA Cup 3rd round against Doncaster tomorrow. Good luck to them. We retain our 5-point lead over Stourbridge, but they drop to 7th, out of the play-off zone.

We filtered out of the ground under the War Memorial Arch. I had an overall sense of satisfaction - about the performance, the result, KD's stunning equaliser, the occasion, the behaviour of both sets of fans, and what a good day it had been amongst so many Yeltzfolk and friends. It's just a shame more could not have been there, but I was very grateful that I was.

December

Tuesday 3 December 2024, Leamington FC Vs Halesowen Town FC – Birmingham Senior Cup Round 2

There was a lovely surprise on Monday, when ITV Central News' sports reporter Dan Salisbury-Jones announced his goal of the weekend. Usually, this spot would be reserved for a strike from a player from a local Premier or Football League team. But this week it went to our very own Kieren Donnelly for his wonder goal on Saturday against Stourbridge.

But not only that, also the brilliant Tom Cartwright from Radio Halesowen Town got a shout out too, for his spontaneously passionate commentary on the goal. It was a great moment for KD and Tom, who have both flourished in their respective roles this season. A good start to the week.

Looking at the meagre balance of my bank account, I was pondering whether to go to Leamington for this fixture. I had a hankering to go back to the New Windmill Ground. This is because a quarter of a century ago, in 2000, I played in the very first competitive game there. At the time Leamington FC, now of the National League North, had reformed, after ceasing to play football in 1988.

I asked Kenny if he was going, which meant not only the company of my wonderful son, but an inexpensive car journey of only 45 minutes. But he said he had too much university work to do. My fatherly side won over, and I said, "Good attitude son, you get your work done, there will be plenty of other games to watch." But the football mate in me wanted to say, "F*ck that right off pal, let's go and watch the Yeltz!"

I have not had a car since before the COVID pandemic, as my last one conked out shortly before the first lockdown. Pre-COVID I had to travel to an office, but I now work from home full-time. So, I never replaced my car, as I do not generally need one, or the expense. And working from home suits me fine. It means I mostly do not have to leave Halesowen, other than watching Villa, Yeltz away, or going on holiday.

No supporters' coach was advertised for this game, for what is now seen as the least prestigious cup competition the club enters. And no-one else I knew was going, to get a lift. So, it would have meant public transport. Which would not have been too bad if the New Windmill Ground is in Leamington Spa town centre, as that means a bus 8 miles to Birmingham, and a train 25 miles to Leamington. But the ground is in the sticks, 4 miles out of town – meaning taxis either end, bumping up the cost considerably. So, I dejectedly gave up the ghost on this one.

Our landlord popped round to see us on Tuesday morning. Lisa was at work, so I hosted him. As ever, it was delightful to see him, because he is a lovely man, a couple of decades my senior, and wonderful landlord. And an Aston Villa fan, to boot. He'd had some bad news, which means in the longer term he might want to sell the house. I felt sad for him because of his news, but also because in the coming months we'll probably have to find a new property to let. We love it here, with the town being a 5-minute walk away, and the countryside literally over the road.

After work I went to Roberto's Bar for a consoling pint, but the news there was no better. Roberto reported that profit margins were tight in an increasingly tough environment for the licenced trade. He said it's busy enough on weekends, but like many pubs, clubs, and bars, trade is too quiet on weekdays. Looking around, after the other usual teatime regulars had gone, only me, Neddy, and Garry sat around the bar, with the odd person drifting in and out.

It was demoralising to think that this magical, little, cozy bar, meeting place for so many of my friends, full of wonderful beer, people, and bar staff, might be lost if things do not pick up. But Roberto is running a business, not a charity, and it is an increasingly difficult time for publicans. Sure, we are blessed with other great beer pubs in Halesowen. But none as good as this bar. If the worst happened and Roberto's shut, the regulars from here will not simply descend on another establishment en masse. They will disperse across several pubs and bars, meaning the community will be lost.

I distracted myself from those depressing thoughts by looking at the Yeltz line up at Leamington on Facebook. It was very much a scratch team, with Mini Macca being the only player in the line-up who started last Saturday. Even coach Martin Riley, and keeper coach Lewis Solly, were in the starting 11.

So, when we went 1-0 down to a Tim Berridge goal on 38 minutes, it could have been a long night. But in a spirited performance, youth team player Ryan Fletcher equalised just after the break, and Yeltz held the score to 1-1 for the duration of the game. It was a shame that Leamington won the penalties tie breaker 6-5. Martin Riley, after a reportedly fine game, hit the bar with his spot kick.

With no more cup distractions, it's 100% focus on the league campaign, and the push for promotion. Starting with Stamford at the Grove on Saturday. And hopefully by then my spirits will have lifted from what has been a melancholy Tuesday. Nothing is permanent, everything passes – our home, Roberto's Bar, my playing career, even life itself. Which is why we need to enjoy things when we can. So, I'm embracing this season, and all the precious games it brings, with all the grace they deserve.

Friday 6 December 2024 – The rumour mill

Strong rumours are circulating that Tamworth, of the National League, want to sign Jordan Ponticelli. Apparently, the player signed for the Yeltz on a non-contact basis. If that is true, he is free to move at any time, after a 7-day notice from the interested club has expired. And we will not receive a fee. Ponticelli probably agreed to join us on a non-contact basis to give him the freedom to move if a bigger club comes in.

There is no doubt that Ponticelli can play at higher levels. I guess that we all knew that he would move on from us, sooner or later. But we had hoped he might see the season out with us and help us to promotion. Then, you never know, in a higher division he might stay.

But the 8 goals he has scored for us in 9 games was always going to attract attention, added to his ex-League pedigree. If Ponticelli leaves, Russ Penn will need to replace him ASAP. Especially given that Nick Clayton Phillips also decided to move on this week, after a short stay with the club.

I suppose tomorrow will be telling – if Tamworth have put in 7-days' notice, it's unlikely he'll be in the squad. If that happens, it seems the rumours are true, and he's off.

POSTPONED - Saturday 7 December 2024, Halesowen Town FC Vs Stamford AFC - Southern League Premier Central

Aston Villa Vs Southampton – Premier League

Quite a few weeks ago, Phil from London contacted me to say that a gentleman from Halesowen was advertising an archive of Yeltz programmes on eBay. Phil wanted to buy them, but there was a hitch, as the seller wanted the buyer to pick them up. So, Phil asked Lisa and I if we would fetch the programmes and store them at ours until he could get them. Of course, we agreed. 'There's not too many,' Phil informed us.

We went to the seller's house at lunchtime. He is a venerable, older gent named Charles, who followed the Yeltz home and away for many years and still pops to the Grove. He turned out to be a Villa fan too, so we hit it off immediately. He also showed interest in my non-League playing career, knowing all the clubs. If I had not had to go back to work, I could have happily whiled away the afternoon chatting about football. We had only scratched the surface of our common interests during our fleeting meeting.

'Not too many' turned out to be a dozen shoe boxes worth of programmes, and also 4 big plastic bags full. They have occupied a space in our entrance hall, which has not really been an issue - until now. This particular space is where a secondary, tall, slim, Christmas tree is due to go. We are keen on getting the trimmings up within the next week or so, as the festive season is fast approaching.

So, it was time for a quid pro quo. Phil said he was thinking of coming up on the train from London for this game, primarily to visit his Dad, who is in a care home. But being close to Christmas, hotel prices have risen to a prohibitive price. I said to Phil that he's more than welcome to stay at mine – just as long as he brings an empty suitcase, to clear out some of the programmes. We had a deal. Christmas would not be cancelled after all.

But like the Biggleswade game back on 23 November, the vagaries of the great British weather came into play. Both Yeltz and Villa were set to kick-off at 3, but with Yeltz-loving Phil up from the Smoke, there was no decision for me to make – I was going to the Grove. But the weekend forecast was dire, with storm Darragh already in full swing.

Earlier in the week I'd bequeathed my Villa season ticket for today's game to Kenny's cousin, Mollie. So, on Friday, to stave off inclement weather, I wanted to do whatever the opposite of the rain dance is, to help ensure the Yeltz game was not called off. In the absence of any other ideas, I decided that was to sling a few pints down my neck on Friday night with Phil, and hope for the best.

But that did not work. On Saturday morning the Yeltz confirmed that the game was postponed, due to a waterlogged pitch. So, we'll have to wait and see regarding the Ponticelli rumours. But now I was ticketless for the Villa game. If ever there is a storm Dom, I sincerely hope it's the mildest one on record, and it leads to no football matches being postponed or abandoned.

I did not want to pay upwards of £65 for a ticket to the Villa game, especially as I could have gone to for free with my season ticket. And it would have been ungentlemanly to snatch my ticket back off Mollie. And besides, I would not be standing with Kenny, and the other regulars by us, in the Holte End, which is half the fun. Also, my finances were not in great shape, and I'd yet to buy any Christmas presents, being too engrossed by all matters football. I chided myself for not having had the foresight to check the weather forecast earlier in the week.

There was one last glimmer of desperate hope. I contacted Big Rich, who stands next to me in the Hotle End, to see if he had a spare ticket. He has a few season tickets for him and his family.

We call him Big Rich to differentiate him from Little Rich, who stands behind us. It's a peculiarity of being a regular football fan that you can see somebody at every home game for years and know very little about them. Not even their surname. That's the case with Little Rich, and others around us. If Little Rich decided to stop going to Villa Park, it would be the end of our association. After years of enjoying his company and repartee, he'd be gone from our lives into the wilderness, with no way of contacting him. When you think about it, it's an odd long-term acquaintanceship to have with someone.

Anyway, incredibly Big Rich, who's a diehard fan, said he was not going to the game, because he has too much work on, and I could have his ticket. I was absolutely chuffed. It not only meant I could go, but I could stand next to Kenny too. It could not be better. I was so delighted and relieved that I almost felt like I owed the forever generous Big Rich my life.

Kenny was going straight to the game from his girlfriend's house. I decided not to tell him the good news about my ticket, preferring to surprise him. And it was worth it when I saw the priceless look and smile on his face, when he saw me standing there in our normal spot.

The game itself was a poor one, Villa overcoming bottom of the table Southampton by a single goal, in dreadful conditions. It was bitterly cold, with a biting wind blowing into the Hotle End. There were some empty seats around the ground, unusual, as Villa Park is normally packed out these days. But some fans had probably looked at the weather and thought better of it.

But I stood there on the Holte End in dreamy wonder at the beauty of it all. A freezing football ground on a

Saturday afternoon in the English winter, standing in our usual spot with Kenny, watching one of our beloved teams. I might have been physically cold, but I had a warm glow all over. It was a magical, life affirming moment, and I could not have been happier.

I used to play football with a talented left-back, Paul Tomlinson, who started his career at Sheffield United. They used to have an old, Scottish, coach. On cold, wintery training days, when the players did not want to leave the warmth of the changing rooms, the coach would shout into the freezing sleet, "Oh, aye, it's good to be alive!" I did not shout that at Villa Park today, but those prophetic words were ringing loud and true in my mind.

Although I enjoyed myself in the Arctic conditions at Villa Park, it was good to get back to the warmth of home. Lisa, Kenny, and I cosied up with a film and Chinese takeaway, and when Lisa customarily fell asleep, we watched *Match of the Day*. 63-year-old Gary Lineker will step down as presenter of the show at the end of this season. He is every bit as brilliant as a broadcaster as he was as a goal scoring centre forward.

For the first time, when Lineker was interviewing Brentford boss Thomas Frank, I thought he has started to look his age. So, as much as I'll miss him as an irreplaceable host, maybe it is time for a change for him. Let's hope the BBC see sense, and appoint the natural replacement, the accomplished Mark Chapman.

It shocked me when I read that Lineker has been the show's presenter for 25 years. That would have been around the same time when I played the first competitive game at Leamington's New Windmill Ground. And Leamington are soon to move on to a new ground too. Again, life moves on, things change. We get older, and we like to think we get wiser. But clearly that's not the case with me. If it was, I would have checked the weather forecast before I gave away my Villa ticket.

Tuesday 10 December 2024, Royston Town FC Vs Halesowen Town FC - Southern League Premier Central

On Sunday Kenny's team, Kidderminster United, had a cup match. Despite storm Darragh, the game was never in doubt because it was played on an artificial pitch - they do have their uses. Kenny was disappointed to be sub, and together with 2 other substitutes, he had the unenviable position of coming on at half time with his team 4-0 down. A thankless task, if ever there was one.

But Kidderminster scored to rekindled hope. Then in no small part due to Kenny's inspiring contribution, incredibly they clawed it back to 4-4, before eventual penalties. When the manager asked who fancied a spot kick, Kenny quickly thrust his hand in the air. It was his first ever shoot out.

Out of the dozens of ways you can take a penalty, his choice was erringly uncanny - because it was exactly the same way I that I took spot kicks in my playing days. A glance to the keeper's right, and a slight feint, both to mislead him, followed by firmly side footing the ball into the bottom corner of the keeper's left. It worked for me in 2 cup finals and other shootouts, and I'm glad to report it worked for Kenny too. His team won the tiebreaker 4-3 to progress to the semi-finals.

The thing is, Kenny never saw me take a penalty, with it being prior to his birth, and there is no footage of me taking one. Also, I've never talked about my penalty technique either. It's like these things are innate - like father, like son.

The question is, if Yeltz get a penalty tonight, will Jordan Ponticelli be taking it, or are the rumours true that he is off to Tamworth. When the starting 11 was announced on Facebook, to the relief of Yeltzfolk, Ponticelli was in it. KD was not, as he's suspended after accumulating too many disciplinary points, following his booking at Stourbridge.

Ponticelli's inclusion in the team leads to 3 potential possibilities. Firstly, the rumours are untrue. Secondly, Russ Penn persuaded the striker to play one last game before leaving, as KD is suspended. Or, thirdly, Tamworth have approached the Yeltz to speak to the player, but Ponticelli has decided to stay at the Grove – maybe we have offered him the carrot of a lucrative contract. So, effectively, it's a waiting game to see if he's in the squad for the Barwell game on Saturday, when the 7-day notice period will have passed.

Ponticelli's inclusion was not the only boost for us ahead of this game. Kettering lost to Barwell last night, with veteran, journey man striker Leroy Lita scoring the winner. This means if we win tonight, it puts us level on points with Kettering, with them having a game in hand. But we still have to play them at their place in January. Before the game Royston sat 17th in the league, so there was cause for optimism. Though midweek long-distance trips in part time football can prove tough.

A few weeks ago, I did have designs on going to this game. With it being close to Christmas, I had a mind to treat myself. And with the supporter's coach departing from the Grove at 4pm, it was do-able if I finished work a little early. But as the game got closer, the financial realities kicked in, and as I plan on travelling to Barwell on Saturday, I need to keep my pennies back for that.

On Halesowen Town Radio it sounded like we had the far better of the first half, without being able to force a goal. It felt like we were going to kick on after the break and push for 3 points. We started the second half well. But then the referee gave captain Ryan Wynter a straight red card, following a challenge on a Royston player. About an hour had gone.

A month ago, we went down to 10 men against Sudbury, with the scores level, and we went on to win the game. So, all did not feel lost. But it sounded like the home team had wrestled the momentum. As the clock ticked towards the closing minutes, 0-0 was looking like a good away result. That was until the 89th minute, when Royston's Ben Weyman met a cross and headed past Dan Platt to snatch the winner. It was 1-0 to Royston at full-time.

The loss ends our undefeated league run of 5 wins and a draw, that stretched back until September. We remain in 2nd, still 3 points behind Kettering, with them having a game in hand. Telford who are 3rd are on the same points as us, with a game in hand too. We play both away soon, in what will be an important period.

But first, Saturday at Barwell, and it's Christmas party time. Well, it is for me, Newty, and Kenny at any rate. Our Yeltz Christmas party day evolved because both Newty and I realised we had not had any Christmas parties in our diaries for years. Whereas both our other halves have many, so we decided to invent one of our own. Kenny is naturally invited.

Watching Yeltz away, with beer either side of it, and a breakfast thrown in for good measure, seems as good an idea as any for a party. And it seems to encapsulate the spirit of Christmas. Dressing up in festive gear is optional – but none of us do or ever will. This year we chose Barwell. They have an artificial surface, so the game should not be called off. Like I say, plastic pitches have their uses.

Saturday 14 December 2024, Barwell FC Vs Halesowen Town FC - Southern League Premier Central

Our party spirits were dampened a little on Friday when the club announced that Jordan Ponticelli has left. The inevitable has come to pass. Well, fair play to him, it looks like he did play one last game at Royston after all, to help Russ Penn out, with KD being suspended.

I realised I had to quickly shake off this disappointment. So, on my lunch break I went on my exercise bike for a 20-minute blast and watched

Kidderminster Harriers boss Phil Brown's preview interview for their game against Radcliffe. The problem is this interview usually lasts 13 minutes, frustratingly leaving 7 minutes to fill before I get off my bike.

Brown was in a good mood. He has just been announced as National League North manager of the month for November, oddly halfway through December. He has an endearing interview technique of replying to the interviewer by asking himself a question, and then answering it. Example: "How serious am I taking the FA Trophy? I said to you before Trevor, and I'm going to say it again, when it's got FA attached to it, it means it's a serious competition. When it's got Wembley attached to it, it is a proper competition."

On Friday evening I went with Kenny to see legendary Villa European Cup winning keepers Jimmy Rimmer and Nigel Spink. It was 'an evening with' event at a local social club. My thoughtful son had bought the tickets for my Christmas present.

The event started at 8.30pm, leaving a problematic 3 ½ hours to fill once I'd finished work. Problematic, because once my working week is done, I'm dog tired. Usually, Lisa and I flop on the sofa on Fridays, and have an early night. My batteries are then recharged for football on Saturday.

Kenny pulled up on the drive at 6, and I frog marched the poor lad straight back out of the house, knowing otherwise I'd be asleep within 10 minutes. Wetherspoons, and cheap, hearty food beckoned. Being a vibrant 20-year-old full of vim, Kenny does not understand my struggles as a middle-aged man being in the red zone on a Friday evening. But then, I do not think he much cared, as he got a free meal and pint out of me.

It was good to listen to Rimmer and Spink and reminisce at the event. But there's a part of me that feels that the past should remain there. I feel a little uncomfortable dredging up yesteryear and the emotions it stirs, even when some of those memories are, on the face of it, happy ones. It's hard to compartmentalise something like Villa winning the league title in 1981, without other elements of your life at that time subconsciously creeping in too. Which is why for the most part, I concentrate on the present and the immediate future.

The immediate future today was focussing on getting to Barwell with Newty and Kenny, then the Yeltz winning. The first bit was relatively straightforward. After breakfast and a beer back in the Spoons, a bus took us to Birmingham, then a train to Nuneaton, which I liked, as it reminds me of Kidderminster. A taxi completed the journey to Barwell.

I could happily do a weekend away in Nuneaton. This might seem like an unusual comment to many people. But Lisa and I often go away to provincial towns or villages in the greater Midlands, for a well-earned break. All we need to keep us happy is a sprinkling of decent beer places – pubs, brewery tap houses, micropubs, bottle shops – a restaurant or two, and the odd place of interest. Bright lights, crowds, heat, and beaches are not really for me, so Nuneaton in midwinter sounds heavenly. I wonder if there's a 'Nuneaton in midwinter' tourist information brochure?

Going through the turnstiles at Barwell's Kirkby Road ground, it did not seem 5 minutes since Kenny and I were there in March, last season. In Russ Penn's first game in charge, we lost 2-0. At non-League grounds you are often close to the pitch, and on that day the vibes were that the camp was not a happy one. Fast forward to today, and the turnaround is striking. A team sitting second in the table, united in team spirit, and other than a blip midweek at Royston, in fine form.

The fine form did not take too long to rekindle. Before 20 minutes had elapsed, skipper Ryan Wynter had scored 2 goals off set pieces, after a great start by the Yeltz. The score remained 2-0 at the break, but in truth it could have been a lot more.

In the second period Barwell grew into the game, without creating much. Then Yeltz started to take control again, spurred on by the vocal fans, including Kenny and I. Despite clearly enjoying himself, Newty refused to be drawn into the singing. He preferred to retain his miserable demeanour, despite the festive time of year.

With less than 10 minutes to go, Musa Ceesay smashed the ball home to kill the home side off. He did a fetching dance towards us Yeltz fans, and even Newty could not hold back a beaming smile. It was a jubilant moment, which meant our Christmas party day now could not be spoilt. The 3 points were ours.

But better was to follow. Minutes later, KD twisted two defenders inside out, before sliding the ball past the keeper. It was his 17th of the season, and his 9th successive goal in the league. Not satisfied, in the last-minute Conor Tee made it 5-0 to complete an absolute rout - on the day when some were concerned about goals, with Ponticelli having left the club. In that moment, in the dark and creeping cold, with my son and best mate, in a village in the wilds of Leicestershire, with about another 150 Yeltzfolk, I could not have been happier.

After the game, the club house was packed, but not uncomfortably so. We decided to watch Nottingham Forest Vs Aston Villa there on TV, because last season the people there had been so friendly and accommodating to Kenny and I. It was a lovely, familiar, warm feeling to be in a buzzing clubhouse on a Saturday teatime, beer in hand, with the game done, and now only talk and laughter remaining. It reminded Newty and I of our longed-for playing days, and we felt at ease, at home.

After the Villa game the trip from Barwell back to Halesowen seemed to go quickly, and predictably we ended up in Roberto's Bar. Despite there being only one more Saturday before Christmas, we were greeted by only a smattering of my fellow regulars, huddled around the bar. Given Roberto's recent comments, I worry about the seductive little bar's future.

As the clock was ticking on, and as he was playing football in the morning, Kenny decided to go home to bed. I'd be joining Kenny in the morning, but only as a spectator. So, with our football playing days behind us,

Newty and I stayed on for a few more drinks. The laughter-filled time passed quickly, and before I knew it, there was just me, and a fellow Horton – Jacob, the brilliant, young barman – and a clock that read well past midnight. Time was up on another annual festive Yeltz awayday.

Getting up on Sunday to go and watch Kenny play football was testing, to say the least. It would have been easy to pull over the duvet and give it a miss. But for all my failings in life, I have at least tried to be a good father – though I guess Kenny would be the best judge of that.

Kenny's team had only lost once all season, scoring many goals, and they generally played entertaining football. So, together with the fresh air, that seemed like as good a remedy for grogginess as any. In a defensive horror show, they got thumped 7-0. In the words of Willie Nelson, 'The party's over.'

Saturday 21 December 2024, Halesowen Town FC Vs Redditch United FC - Southern League Premier Central

The job I do, to earn money to go to football matches, is a writer and editor of health information for a charity. This week our head of IT held a workshop on artificial intelligence, or AI as it is known. We went through our – complicated - AI policy, had a discussion and Q&A's, and he gave us a demonstration of an AI tool. Whether we like it or not, AI will play increasing parts in all our lives. And I'm guessing my type of work will soon look radically different.

As a writer I am used to a blank screen in front of me, my mind to create ideas, and places to research information. AI seems to be changing that basic format for writers, and in some instances, there might not be a need for writers at all.

But AI cannot replicate everything - like a game of football. Sure, there has been changes in football, but the fundamentals of the modern game have remained largely the same. And I hope that continues to be the case long into the future, and that it is played and watched by real people, out in the fresh air.

AI can seemingly write anything you tell it to. But could AI write about one man's experiences of following the Yeltz for the season? Could it go to the games? I've never seen AI on the East Terrace or in the Shed End, eating cheesy chips. Granted, some Stourbridge fans could do with a dose of artificial intelligence. But even their individuality and humanity cannot ultimately be replaced by the intangible clever dick that is AI. And I hope that does not offend any Stourbridge supporters named Alexa.

The answer to 'could AI write about one man's experiences of following the Yeltz for the season?' appears to be no. I challenged a well-know, paid for, AI tool to 'Write me a short story about one man's experiences of watching Halesowen Town football club's games so far this 2024/25 season.' My expectation was that all the factual stuff would be correct, as that's all easily available on the web, but the experiential content would be a bit rubbish. I was wrong. Even the factual information was incorrect - scorelines, teams in our league, names of players. So, maybe there is still a need for people like me to record our aimless mental ramblings.

I am from the generation that bridges the analogue and digital worlds. I grew up with print newspapers, landline telephones, transistor radios, 3 TV channels, roadmaps, and the A-Z system for half times scores at football. I'm glad I have the benefit of seeing all the technological changes in the context of the old world. So, for example, I know how to write without the benefits of an AI tool, though reading this book, you might beg to differ. Or I could navigate myself to a cottage in Cornwall without a Sat Nav. But AI is out of Pandora's box, and there is no going back.

The only box I was interested in today is 18 yards long and 44 yards wide, and I was hoping Yeltz goalkeeper Platty was going to command it. But first, Kenny and I had Villa Park to attend to. Villa were playing Manchester City at 12.30. So, to maximise our football, we decided to go to that match first, then dash to the Grove to take in the second half of the Yeltz game.

Villa convincingly beat Man City 2-1, with Halesowen lad Morgan Rogers scoring the second goal. It was incredible to see the sudden fall from grace of the demoralised looking City players and manager, Pep Guardiola. They have now gone 10 games in all competitions without a win, losing 8 of those. In football, no team is impregnable, which is one of the multitudes of reasons why we love the game so much.

Leaving Villa Park in Kenny's car, our attentions turned towards the Yeltz game. Team news told us that new dual registration signing Jamie Willets, from Tamworth FC, was in at centre half for the suspended skipper, Ryan Wynter. Wynter joined the Halesowen Town Radio commentary team for the day.

I asked Kenny to remind me to go to the James Grove Lounge after the game, to pay Jackie for our coach tickets for the Boxing Day trip to Telford. We discussed whether to go to Bedford next Saturday. Kenny said he cannot go. After committing to Telford on Boxing Day, if I make the trip to Bedford two days later, it probably will not go down well with Lisa at this festive time of year.

As we travelled to the Grove, we learnt from the commentary that Ryan Wollacott had headed Yeltz in front, off a Conor Tee corner, after 12 minutes. Only for us to concede a minute later, Redditch's Johnny Johnston being the scorer. From the clues you pick up on the radio, it did not sound like a free-flowing game.

Before the second half kicked off, we were comfortably in situ in our usual spot on the East Terrace, opposite the Screwshop billboard on the opposite touchline. There was a good festive crowd inside the Grove, announced as 1,259. But this had not considered the late comers Kenny and I, so the actual attendance was 1,259+2 big nosed Hortons.

As my intuition had picked up from the radio commentary, the game was scrappy, with the blustery conditions and heavy pitch not helping. Redditch were rugged and combative, and a slightly different animal to the one we had beaten 3-0 in the FA Trophy in October. With ex-Yeltz man Matt Clarke back as their boss, they were hard to break down and had a steely determination.

But I always felt that with the quality we have in the team, we just needed one moment to score a goal to snatch the game. With a few minutes to go Hickman played a decent ball up the line, which KD squared to Tee, who was 8 yards out with the ideal chance to score. It felt like it could be that moment. But a Redditch defender put in a valiant block on Tee's shot to avert the danger. As the game drew to a close a point did not seem too bad, because Kettering were also drawing with Spalding. So, it would mean the table would remain unchanged.

As the contest was exhaling its final breath, midfielder Josh Smile picked up the ball on the halfway line. He Cruyff turned a Redditch midfielder, and drove forward, before being fouled about 25 yards out. Wideman Conor Tee stepped up to take the free kick. Astonishingly, he delivered the ball over the wall, and it dipped beyond the gloves of the flying keeper Ollie Taylor, sweetly into the net. The Grove erupted in unfettered jubilant celebrations. With less than a minute on the clock, the game was won 2-1.

Poor Ollie Taylor has had the short end of the stick against the Yeltz in recent weeks. That's because he was also the keeper for Stourbridge when KD scored his remarkable equaliser a couple of weeks ago. There are two oddities to note about Taylor. Firstly, there is a photograph of him on my office wall – albeit he's plucking the ball out the net at the Victoria Ground, Bromsgrove, after Yeltz had just scored, with Kenny and I celebrating in the background. Secondly, his father - Maik Taylor, the former Fulham, Birmingham City, and Northern Ireland goalkeeper – shares the same birthday as me, 4 September 1971.

The final whistle led to a rapturous reception for the players after another memorable win. We are now only one point behind Kettering, having played a game more. But before Kenny and I could raise a glass in the warmth of Roberto's Bar, to what had been a spellbinding day of football, we had to go and pay Jackie. We paid for our Boxing Day coach tickets to Telford, and I was about to walk away, but I hesitated. "I tell you what Jackie," I said, "put me down for Bedford away next Saturday." Carpe diem – or in the English translation, 'Seize the day.'

Thursday 26 December 2024, AFC Telford United Vs Halesowen Town FC - Southern League Premier Central

The last time I was in Telford it was also at Christmas time, Christmas Eve to be more precise. We went to the Crown Inn at Oakengates to watch a favourite band of ours, the Percy Veer band, for Lisa's birthday. But as there were no B&Bs or hotels in Oakengates, we stayed in nearby Telford.

After finishing our meal, we tried to get a taxi from the restaurant in Telford to the Crown Inn, about 2 miles away. Uber does not operate there, so we tried to book a cab with a local equivalent. But it proved difficult. We called several other taxi firms, but the wait times were too long. There were no buses, so I was starting to gee Lisa up for a brisk walk. "It'll do us good. We can walk our dinner off." This was received about as well as a fox in a hen house.

Then I had a flash of inspiration. The train station was not too far away, and you often find taxis there. There was a single taxi, unoccupied by passengers, and the driver was pulling away. I frantically hobbled after him, waving my arms. Thankfully he stopped and agreed to take us to Oakengates. The elderly driver said he had finished his shift and was about to head off home. We expressed our deep gratitude.

As the journey progressed, and we chatted to the driver, something suddenly struck me - how on earth would we get back from the village of Oakengates to Telford at midnight? At that very moment the driver asked us, "Do you want me to pick you up later?" I replied, "That's really kind of you, but you said you have finished your shift?" "Oh, don't worry about that," he said, "I'll go home, have me tea, watch a bit of telly, and get you later." At midnight the driver was good to his word and was waiting for us, and of course, we tipped him handsomely.

The lessons here were twofold. Firstly, the kindness of people is universal, and every time I experience it, it leaves me with warmth and wonder. Secondly, in Halesowen, we are spoilt not only with public transport links, but the availability of taxis too. If I order an Uber, it will invariability arrive at my house, or elsewhere, within minutes.

It's the same following Yeltz away on public transport. Planning is the key. The Southern League Premier Central hosts some of the sleepier backwaters in

England, so you need to do your research before you set off. But today Kenny and I opted for the club coach, with it being Boxing Day, and therefore no trains. The operation runs under the masterful command of Jackie, who works hard to ensure all runs smoothly. The flat fee for all trips, far and wide, is a very reasonable £15.

In this crucial top of the table clash at the New Bucks Head Stadium, there was no kindness on offer in the gloomy mist. We started the game 4 points ahead of them, having played a game more. But from the kick off, it was the home side that was the more dominant. And they made that tell on 20 minutes, when Matthew Stenson scored following the award of a controversial free kick.

Yeltz found it hard to get going, and when Telford got a corner before the break, I feared the worst. We have a poor track record defending set pieces over the previous couple of seasons. I was right to be anxious, because despite the suspicion of a foul on Platty, the ball ended up in the back of the net, and the goal was given. Ricardo Dinanga was the scorer. 2-0 to Telford at the break.

The second period saw the introduction of newly signed forwards Alex Cameron and Charlie Wragg, the latter on a one-month loan from Walsall. But together with KD, Mini Macca and the other Yeltz players, they had little impact and on a frustrating afternoon, few opportunities were created.

To their credit Telford were mean in defence and sharp in attack, and it was the best individual team performance we had faced this season. It made me reflect that until now they had maybe underachieved, and with our hitherto thin squad, we had possibly overachieved.

The top of the table looks like this: 1st Kettering, P 20 Pts 43; 2nd Yeltz, P 21 Pts 39; 3rd Telford,
P 20 Pts 38; 4th Stratford, P21 Pts 36; 5th Bedford P20 Pts 34.

Redditch at home last Saturday was a high, today, a low. We play Bedford away next Saturday. What will that bring? Well, after cancelling my coach seat, it should bring a highly organised away day on public transport with Kev and Sid.

Saturday 28 December 2024, Bedford Town FC Vs Halesowen Town FC - Southern League Premier Central

I got up in the weekend quiet and darkness at 6.45am, trying not to disturb Lisa. I reflected that thousands of other football fans around the country, who are travelling to away games, would be doing the very same thing. The sacrifice of the Saturday lie in to head out into the cold, to make a 4-legged journey to another provincial footballing outpost was, as ever, fuelled by a mixture of excitement and insanity.

Normally on these trips, I'm the planner. So, on Friday, I went through my usual routines of looking up train times, connections, Uber availability, good pubs etc. On Friday morning I put a briefing of all this information in a text message to Kev, and pressed send. At the very same instant my phone pinged, and I received a

WhatsApp message. It was from Kev, and it contained the very same information. So, Saturday turned out to be a joy, as I did not have to take charge of anything. Kev directed Sid and I to platforms, pubs, and pitches.

So, it was incredible that I managed to make such a mess of the start to the day. Breakfast is a pretty simple routine on these football away days - decide on which Wetherspoons you are meeting in, and tuck into your first meal of the day. We were meeting in the Wetherspoons in New Street station, Birmingham. But as I waited for the bus to Birmingham in Halesowen, I felt hungry and decided I could not go the 40 odd minutes journey without any sustenance. The board said 7 minutes until the bus arrives. I calculated that would give me enough time to rush into Asda, buy a breakfast sandwich, and scoff it before the bus turns up. But as soon as I took a bite of the butty my transport arrived, and you can no longer eat on local buses.

When we got to New Street, I ate the sandwich, which was dry and disgusting, before watching Sid tuck into a hot and hearty plateful of full English delights in Wetherspoons. I chastised myself, because panic buying the sandwich was an inexcusable error from a seasoned campaigner. I thought if the Yeltz players exercise poor judgement in the game, I can hardly criticise them.

And it turned out not to be my only food faux pas of the day. To make up for my sandwich disappointment, I went to buy my customary cheeseburger when we arrived at The New Eyrie stadium. The cheeseburgers were a pricey £6. In the queue next to me was a blue and white scarved man, who I assumed was a fellow

Yeltz fan. I complained to him, "£6 is a bit steep aye it me mon. These Southerners must think wee'm med o' money." He replied, clearly annoyed, in a southern accent, "I think £6 is pretty reasonable, and they are decent quality." I'd forgotten that Bedford Town also play in blue and white – I'd put my foot right in it.

Even though I'd had a breakfast disaster, and subsequently offended a local, the journey to Bedford via Leicester was uncannily seamless. And the time in the pubs with Kev and Sid was pleasant. The only thing that could disrupt the day was the football. And disrupt it did. After conceding in the first 3 minutes to a Ryan Blake goal, after failing to clear, Yeltz rallied and were by far the better team. The pressure eventually told before the break, when Conor Tee both won and dispatched a penalty in fine style. 1-1 at half-time, and we hoped if we continued in the same vein after the break, the 3 points would surely be ours.

But the game quickly turned on its head. Musa Ceesay picked up two quick yellow cards with only 10 minutes gone in the second half and was sent off. The second booking seemed particularly harsh. On the hour mark Yeltz again failed to clear the ball, and Panter scored for Bedford to put them 2-1 up. Panter grabbed his second 5 minutes later, a wonderful curling effort, putting the ball beyond Platt, and the game beyond Yeltz. 3-1 to Bedford.

In the mist and dark of the small, but attractive, New Eyrie stadium, it left us contemplating our first back-to-back league defeats since September. We are still 2nd in the league but if Telford and Bedford win their game in hand, they can jump above us. And we are now

5 points behind Kettering. But at the halfway mark in the season, we have done incredibly well to be where we are, and there is plenty of football still to come. And I, for one, am optimistic. But the silly mistakes must end - like choosing a stale sandwich in preference to a freshly cooked breakfast.

January

Wednesday 1 January 2025, Halesowen Town FC Vs Bromsgrove Sporting FC - Southern League Premier Central

This was a game that I knew I could not attend, as Lisa and I were going away over New Year to Newark with friends, Paul and Teresa. I could hardly complain, as Lisa is more than understanding of my football going habits.

Last New Year we were away in Shrewsbury, and Yeltz were away to Alvechurch on New Year's Day. Back then, I did not simply concede that I could not go to the game. Instead, I kept thinking of schemes of how I could get to Alvechurch, and back to Shrewsbury, with the minimum of travel time, so that Lisa, Paul, and Teresa would have hardly noticed I had gone. I pursued train timetables and even considered a very expensive Uber directly back. So, it was to my great relief that the game was postponed.

The Alvechurch game was rescheduled for a Tuesday night and Newty, Kenny, and I went along. We sheltered from the pre-match rain and cold in the renown real ale pub the Weighbridge, on the canal in the village. Given the inclement weather, the convivial surroundings, and the quality of the beer, we did not really want to leave, but leave we must, as kick off was getting close.

As we approached Alvechurch's Lye Meadow's ground, unusually cars were not parked on the side of the road. We saw a steward at the entrance of the club car park and made enquiries. His message was simple: "Game's off mate." The lesson was simple – check social media before you leave the pub. To complete the saga, Kenny and I eventually watched the Yeltz win 2-0 at Lye Meadow on a cold, dry subsequent Tuesday night with a workmanlike performance.

Today, I resigned myself to the fact that I could not go to the Yeltz game. Newark to Halesowen and back was not feasible, and it did not seem healthy to have such madcap thoughts of escape. I thought though that Paul and I could at least venture out to watch some local New Year's Day football. This was not without precedent, as we've done this before on a previous New Years Day, and Lisa and Teresa happily sat in a pub for the afternoon.

My research found that there are plenty of non-League teams in and around Newark. But most of them had no games, and the ones that did were playing away. This seemed incredibly unfair. Because in my playing days we always had to fulfil a New Year's Day fixture with bleary eyes, and a lot of those were morning kick-offs.

Despite me not being able to attend the Yeltz game, I wanted us to win more than any other game this season. The reason being, Kenny, who was attending, had just split up with his girlfriend. He was very down in the dumps about it and needed something to lift his spirits.

Kenny and I are usually together on the terraces game in, game out, watching both the Yeltz and Aston Villa. And yet the time I could really do with being with him, the hand of fate has me in Newark. But bless the lovely lot of Kenny's Mom, Sally, her partner Andy, and Kenny's little bother George, and little sister Zoe. Because they wrapped the warm scarf of love around him and stood with him at the Grove.

But the Yeltz offered poor Kenny no solace. They went down to a 2-0 defeat, after goals by Jamie Meddows and Fin Holmes, on 54 and 70 minutes respectively. Kenny said we had a lot of the ball and knocked it around nicely, but did not create many proper chances. Defensively we sounded poor. Russ Penn: "We shouldn't be conceding the way we are, it's really poor. We just aren't ruthless enough in the defence at the moment, and we are just conceding way too many goals for my liking. We need to change it and do so quick."

But there was one incident, which sounded like one of the funniest things that has happened in the long history of the Grove, that caused belly laughs for all spectators. A tubby male streaker ran on the pitch during the game and made his way to the edge of the 18-yard box, dropped his jeans, and revealed his bare bottom to the Yeltz faithful.

Stalwart Yeltz steward, known to all as the Ferret, was not having any of it. The Ferret is no longer a spring chicken and must be one of the shortest stewards in the whole of football. But he did not let either of these things put him off, and he bolted from the Shed End to the pitch invader, spitting feathers as he went, his feet slipping in the mud.

When he reached the offender, Ferret attempted a rugby tackle. But the streaker dropped a shoulder and slipped his clutches. The Ferret lost his footing and landed unceremoniously in the mud, to uproarious laughter from all 4 sides of the ground. The pitch invader was eventually apprehended by burlier stewards, but not after revealing his bum one more time to the Shed End.

On a more serious note, this is the first time we have had 3 defeats on the bounce under Russ Penn's management. It leaves us 4th in the table, 5 points behind our next opponents, Kettering, who are top, and they still have a game in hand. But Telford and Stamford both have games in hand too and could jump above us if they win them. So, we quickly need to get back to winning ways.

More importantly, on returning from Newark I saw Kenny and immediately hugged him. Pretty much every time we see each other we embrace, but it is a brief momentary man hug. This time the coming together was deep, lasting, and loving. He needed it. Hell, I needed it. I had been worried about him and just wanted to see him and chat things through face to face, as things are not the same on the phone. He's going away with his mates for a few days to Budapest, and hopefully the trip is good timing and will lift his spirits. Girlfriends might come and go for him, but some things will always be there – like his family, friends, and Halesowen Town FC.

POSTPONED - Saturday 4 January 2025, Kettering Town FC Vs Halesowen Town FC - Southern League Premier Division Central

Aston Villa FC Vs Leicester City FC – Premier League

With Kettering and Yeltz having occupied the top two spots in the league for weeks, I'd been looking forward to going this game for some time. Latimer Park looks like an attractive ground to visit, and Kettering have been getting a lot of fans through the turnstiles this season. So, it was a mouth-watering fixture. But to save anyone travelling, Kettering sensibly took an early decision to call the game off, due to a frozen pitch.

So, it was off to a cold Villa Park with my brother Warwick to see the Villans beat a struggling Leicester City 2-1. It was not quite the same without Kenny at my side, as he's in Budapest, but an enjoyable victory, nonetheless.

Yeltz benefitted from this round of fixtures without kicking a ball, because Bedford, Stratford, and Stamford lost, and they are all around us in the table. And after 3 losses, maybe a week off to reset and rejuvenate was not such a bad thing.

POSTPONED - Saturday 11 January 2025, Halesowen Town FC Vs Royston Town FC - Southern League Premier Central

Rushall Olympic FC Vs Scunthorpe United FC – National League North

On this FA Cup 3rd round weekend my football watching started with Kenny on Friday night at Villa Park. The 2-1 victory over West Ham, on the club's 150th anniversary game, was a rare FA Cup win.

It was watching FA Cup finals as a young boy in the mid-70's that started my long and lasting love affair with football. It has consumed my life ever since. Even though Villa have got to the final twice in my lifetime, I saw them lose both times – once in the last final at the old Wembley in 2000, and once at the new stadium with Kenny in 2015. So, my dream of us lifting the famous old trophy remains unfulfilled. They say it's the hope that kills you. But I hope I witness Villa winning the FA Cup.

Realistically, with the Arctic conditions this week, the Yeltz game was never going to be on. And a pitch inspection at 9 o'clock on Saturday morning confirmed the postponement. At least the suspense lasted until Saturday morning – a dozen Football League games were called off on Friday. But I was determined to not have a football-less Saturday afternoon, despite the local non-League programme being decimated by the weather.

On Friday I developed a contingency plan, which was to watch Rushall Olympic FC Vs Scunthorpe United

FC in the National League North, as Rushall have an artificial pitch. But it is not unheard of that games on plastic can be called off – indeed Marine Vs Kidderminster fell foul of the freezing weather. So, I had Walsall Vs Tranmere in League 2 as a back-up. The Saddlers seemed confident the game would go ahead.

On Saturday Rushall confirmed on X their game was on, so Kenny and I made our way to Dales Lane. It was an exciting prospect, because I do not think I had been there before, and the two teams made an interesting match-up.

Rushall have worked their way up through the non-League steps. In 2022-23 they got promoted to the National League North for the first time in their history. An incredible achievement for a club from such a small town. Conversely, Scunthorpe have spent most of their existence in the Football League and were even in the Championship not too long ago. Before kick-off Rushall were bottom of the League, and Scunthorpe 3rd, with high hopes of promotion.

I did not know too much about Rushall Olympic before we arrived at Dales Lane, other than their boss is Richard Sneekes, ex-West Brom midfielder. And Wikipedia told me the ground holds 1,400. Kenny and I were impressed by what a wonderful set up the club have. Small but characterful, and everything shipshape. The stadium even boasts a hospitality area where diners can watch the game from the comfort of a well-appointed lounge. And as artificial surfaces go, they have one of the better ones.

All football grounds are different, but non-League grounds really are generally eclectic. As clubs improve and get promoted, bits are added on, so grounds end up higgledy-piggledy and completely unique. And with low stands and terraces you can see big, changing skies, and trees and buildings outside the ground. Inside the stadiums are burger vans, Portakabins, shipping containers, small stands, odd bits of terracing, bars, scaffolding for media, floodlight pylons, and Portaloos. Because of their endearing idiosyncratic charm, for me quirky non-League football grounds are little slices of heaven on Earth.

Also in my life, football grounds, and non-League ones in particular, have always acted as a safe haven. I live with PTSD, so most of the time my mind and thoughts are fearful and frenetic. But when I enter one of these minor theatres of football, I feel calm, at peace, at home. Until the referee blows the whistle to start the game that is, when my pulse rate rises once more - but in a good way. So, over my life as a player, coach, and now a spectator, I've always been drawn to these places, like a moth to a flame.

Once we'd secured our obligatory cheeseburgers – which were a good standard, and a reasonably priced £4 – Kenny and I took up a good position, standing on a terrace near the halfway line. And what a game we witnessed, to warm us in the near sub-zero temperatures.

It quickly became clear that despite being bottom of the league there is nothing wrong with Rushall's spirit and work rate, and they have good quality too. So, after a good opening half hour it was a shame they went 1-0 down to a Danny Whitehall goal, after a defensive error and a suspicion of off-side. But Rushall showed monumental endeavour and refused to lie down. They got their just rewards through an equaliser, on around the hour mark, through substitute striker Ben Wodskou.

Kenny and I were hoping that Rushall could cling on for a draw – but they had other ideas, and with about 20 minutes to go another substitute, Sam Mantom, popped up in the box at the right moment to slot home. Sterling defending for the remaining minutes got the home side over the line for a magnificent 2-1 win, that edged them to within 3 points of safety.

The enthralling game, the heroic win, and the footballing day out generally, was a great therapeutic tonic for Kenny, who is still a little tender after splitting up with his girlfriend. Hopefully he's beginning to appreciate that football is one of the cornerstones of his existence that he will be able to rely on throughout his life. I'm just so fortunate that we have shared so much football together, from me coaching his kids' football teams, to us standing on terraces at countless matches. I cherish every priceless second of it.

This thoroughly entertaining game, at this wonderfully welcoming Black Country football club, re-emphasised an important footballing lesson – if your team is well organised, fit, and play with spirit, you always have a chance. I hope Rushall manage to survive. But even if they do not, I hope to return to Dales Lane soon. Because fate had thrown up an unexpected magical afternoon.

Tuesday 14 January 2025, Halesowen Town FC Vs Stamford FC - Southern League Premier Division Central

Before this game I pondered that it seemed like an age since I had been to the Grove. In reality, it was only just over 3 weeks ago. But that was before Christmas. I've been to 2 away games and missed one home game since, with 2 postponements thrown in. So, my mind deceived me into thinking that my last visit was months ago. So, I was very much looking forward to standing on the East Terrace with Kenny again.

In the context of our season, this game felt pivotal. Before kick-off we were 5th and Stamford 6th, with both teams on the same points and goal difference. So, a win was crucial for us to reignite our season, after recent poor form.

A boost came with news that we have signed 26-year-old midfielder Kacy Butterfield on a season long loan from Basford United. Wikipedia says he not only has experience at a decent non-League level but also has 6 caps for the Bermuda national team. Let's hope that during games he does not go missing.

I do not want to get my hopes up too high with Butterfield. This is because the last international that we signed is the allegedly well paid, but Ill-fated, Adi Yussuf, who has 4 caps for Tanzania. He has since gone out on loan to Redditch, much to the relief of most Yeltzfolk. In fairness to Russ Penn though, other than Yussuf, his signings have been good. And we all know how tricky bringing in new players can be.

Kenny offered to pick me up at 7.15pm for a 7.45pm kick-off. But Lisa was out, so after I finished work, I was just listlessly kicking around the house, waiting to go to the Grove. Eventually I could take it no longer, and I decided to pop down Roberto's Bar for a quick pint. But even there I could not settle, despite talking to friends and pub regulars huddled around the bar. I finished my pint and headed up the Stourbridge Road in the direction of the floodlights, as fast as my worn legs would carry me.

On the face of it, it did not really make a lot of sense to get to the ground so early. I did not even buy a programme to read, or visit the James Grove Lounge, food hut, or club shop. I just stood surveying the two stands and two terraces of my beloved Grove, virtually devoid of fans at that time, watching the players warm up. And it really was a rare moment of pure luxury.

The team news mysteriously revealed that midfield mainstay Todd Parker was not in the squad at all. He was replaced by new man Kacy Butterfield in midfield. The other change saw Ben Cassidy come in at right midfield for Mini Macca, who dropped to the bench. I bumped into old football friend Litch, who informed me that Todd Parker was away on a midweek skiing holiday, as no fixture was due to be played tonight. But this game was rearranged after its previous postponement.

The imposing Butterfield quickly enforced his dominance in the middle, and it was needed against a physical Stamford team. But he can also play too, and he quickly formed a decent partnership with the classy Josh Smile. And it was the latter who capitalised on early Yeltz dominance after just 30 minutes, with a fabulous goal, his first for the club. A corner was cleared to Smile on the edge of the box. He fainted past a defender and moved the ball to his right, then struck a clean diagonal drive across goal, giving the keeper no chance. 1-0 to the Yeltz.

We gave the visitors nothing before the break, but Ben Cassidy gave them a massive problem after it. Following a strong, direct run down the middle of the pitch, beating 3 or 4 players, he was brought down in the box. It gave the referee no option but to point to the spot. Conor Tee confidently dispatched the penalty, extending Yeltz's lead to 2-0, scoring his 9th of the season.

Stamford's reacted with bully boy and long ball tactics, but they did not dent Yeltz's steely resolve. We could have extended our lead on several occasions, with KD and sub Mini Macca missing chances.

It was one of those nights when everybody played well, individually and as a unit. But one player stood out for me, and that was Ben Cassidy. I admired him when he was captain and right-back at Alvechurch, so I was delighted when we signed him in the summer. But despite being a brilliant player at this level, he has found it hard to find a consistent spot in the team. Yet every time he has played, in various positions, he has always played well.

Tonight, Cassidy's dynamism, endeavour, and quality really helped make the difference, and I was pleased for him. It's easy to bang on the manager's door asking for a move if you are not in the team every week. But sometimes it takes a greater strength of character to stick it out and back yourself and have the determination to force your way into the team.

One disturbing thing tonight was the very meagre crowd of 570. For some reason, attendances at the Grove for midweek games are always lower than on a Saturday. But this is the smallest crowd I can remember for quite some time. Especially as none of the local professional teams had games. I hope the small crowd was not because people are losing interest because we have lost the last 3 games. Players need fans' support through thick and thin, not just through the thick.

Saturday 18 January 2025, AFC Sudbury Vs Halesowen Town FC - Southern League Premier Central

The one New Year's resolution that I have made for many years is not to make any New Year's resolutions. But going into 2025 I was mindful that I needed to get a better grip of my budget. I am certainly not a lavish person, and rarely buy clothes, records - or the modern equivalent – or expensive meals. The only clubs I go to are ones with the prefixes of 'football', 'working man's' or 'social.'

I do work for a charity though, with an income to match. So, I need to be more careful about where I spend my pennies. Which meant, no trip to the deep wilds of Suffolk for me today to watch the Yeltz. This is with a view to making the shorter trip to Stratford-Upon-Avon next Saturday, after the home game against Royston on Tuesday.

Instead, Kenny and I popped to Aggborough to watch a rampant Kidderminster Harriers cruise past a laboured Warrington 2-0, to remain top of the National League North. The visitors were lucky to get nil, and in truth Kiddy could have had a bag full after playing some delightful football and creating a plethora of chances.

The afternoon was only marred by me taking a homemade cheese and pickle sandwich to save money. But the bread was dry, and not being a hot snack, it did not cut it on a freezing cold afternoon. Conversely, Kenny purchased a steaming meat pie, which he ate with great gusto. The pies at Kiddy are rightly renown as some of the best in football. If he had still been a young child, I might have commandeered a big bite of it.

The news from Sudbury's King's Marsh stadium via X was that Yeltz were unchanged from Tuesday. But in a sign of how small our squad is, both our first team and goalkeeping coaches, Martin Riley and Lewis Solly, were named as substitutes.

The overall picture of the game seemed to be that Sudbury had the better of the first half. But Russ Penn made a tactical switch at the break, withdrawing striker Alex Cameron, replacing him with midfielder Todd Parker. It worked, and Yeltz wrestled control to such a degree that Sudbury's goalkeeper James Bradbrook was named man of the match, after a string of important saves. But deadlock remained, and the final score ended 0-0.

On Yeltz TV, boss Penn seemed pleased overall: "A point is a fair result at the end of the day, but we were knocking on the door more than them in the second half. I'm delighted with a point to be honest, after losing 3 games over Christmas, to follow it up with 4 points and 2 clean sheets is great, because I think we are looking solid again."

The result leaves us 4th, only 3 points behind leaders Telford, who have played the same number of games. But 2nd place Kettering, who have a point advantage over us, have 2 games in hand. We play them away on Tuesday 25th February.

But first, Royston at home on Tuesday, and we owe them one. In the reverse fixture, not long before Christmas, we had the better of the game before Ryan Wynter was sent off, then we lost 1-0. The memory of that bitter defeat needs to drive the boys on to victory in another mid-weeker at the Grove.

Tuesday 21 January 2025, Halesowen Town FC Vs Royston Town FC - Southern League Premier Central

Kenny and I were excited by a two-legged evening of football, beginning with Monaco Vs Aston Villa in the Champions League on TV, kicking off at 5.45. Following this was the Yeltz game, starting at 7.45. It was going to be tight to get to the Grove for kick-off after the end of the Villa game, but in theory it was achievable by car.

Monaco went into the game in poor form. Conversely, Villa were getting back to their best. A win in this one would pretty much guarantee progression to the next round of the Champions League. But Villa were poor, lost 1-0, and even worse, the game ran over a bit, and Kenny even clocked that half-time took 18 minutes.

This meant that we got to the Grove right on kick-off. But we were scuppered on arrival, because the Stourbridge Road turnstiles were already shut, meaning that we had to go all the way around the ground to the turnstiles on Old Hawne Lane. There we heard the sound that perfectly defines the term 'mixed emotions' – the Yeltz crowd cheered a goal. Mixed because we were delighted that we had scored but frustrated that we had not seen it.

Kenny paid his £9 for student rates and the turnstile operator said, "I'll need to see your student card, we're cracking down." Kenny went to produce his student card on his app, but it would not load. "Ahh, doe worry mate, goo on," gestured the operator. Nazi Germany the Grove is not.

We learned that the Yeltz goal, that a woeful Villa had caused us to miss, was from the ever brilliant, and consistently reliable, Conor Tee. It teed things up nicely. And Tee extended the Yeltz lead on 24 minutes. The ball bounced high in the box. A typically brave Kieren Donnelly got to the ball with his head before the goalkeeper and nodded goalwards. Tee quickly followed up to help the ball into the net for his 11th goal of the season – not bad for a wide man. 2-0. Royston struck back quickly through Harrison Rookard, but it was Yeltz who went in at the break a goal to the good at 2-1.

For the second half we unusually broke with our habit of standing opposite the Screwshop advertising hoarding, and moved down the East Terrace, closer to the Stourbridge Road end. The reason being, the dastardly Royston captain must have won the toss and opted to force the Yeltz to kick towards the Shed End in the first half, as opposed to our favoured second half.

As all football fans know, it is a tradition for the home side to prefer to kick towards their home end in the second half. If the opposition captain does something to disrupt this at the pre-match coin toss, it is seen at best as ungentlemanly, and at worst as despicable.

Moving from our normal spot was not a decision we took lightly. Football fans by nature are superstitious, and Kenny and I are no different. Upsetting the applecart at 2-1 up was a massive risk. But it meant we would get a better view of Yeltz's assaults on the opposition goal. But after the break it turned out the balance of the action was down the Shed End anyway.

The game turned into a battle that was not for the faint hearted. The Yeltz players to a man responded to this with bloody minded conviction. And despite Royston pressure, we had the better chances and should have put the game to bed on at least 2 counter attacking occasions. But the team's resolve was such that Platt's goal was simply not going to be breached. The long-awaited final whistle signalled 3 of the hardest earned points of the season. I could not have been prouder of the players.

These games in deepest, darkest January in many ways are the ones that define a football season. Somehow these precious points, won in the mud and the cold, feel like they are worth more than those gained on beautiful pitches in sunny August. The points count the same of course, but the psychology of them can make a difference.

The other psychological bonus of tonight is that the win sees us go top of the league. Some might say that our position is a little false, as Kettering in 4th have 3 games in hand and are only 2 points behind. But others would roll out the cliché that points in the bag are better than games in hand. Either way, being top of the tree can only be a good thing. So much so, that Kenny and I were duty bound to pop into Roberto's Bar to raise a glass, to mark the occasion.

Despite the customary lull in trade in January that all licenced premises experience, the outlook at Roberto's is less gloomy than forecast a few weeks ago. In fact, our genial host Roberto is fully entitled to say, "Rumours of my bar's demise have been greatly exaggerated." The reason for optimism is down to two things.

Firstly, a swish looking lighted spirits' wrack has been installed behind the bar. Because it was fixed to the wall by my dear friend Neddy, it is only a matter of time before it falls down. But that's not the point. Secondly, Roberto has struck a deal with Nickolls & Perks, wine and spirits merchants, to improve his offering of wines. So, it seems that the future of our bolthole is thriving. Which means I need to continue my service to, and support of, the bar by continuing to visit it as often as possible.

On arrival at Roberto's, I was not interested in his offering of fine wines, I was solely focused on his beer and thawing out my frozen feet. While I was perusing the beer on offer, Roberto asked, "Would you like a mystery beer? £2 for 2/3 pint." As everyone else seemed to be drinking it, it would have been foolish of me to not take up this bargain. It turned out he had to shift the craft beer quickly before it went off, because of a problem with the gas. It was pretty good.

The biggest mystery though, is given our lofty league position, why was there only 512 at the Grove tonight, an even smaller crowd than last Tuesday? I guess there are several contributory factors: it's January, it's cold, there is Champions League football on the TV, and West Brom were on TV too, away at Middlesborough. But nonetheless, it is a poor crowd, given we are having a relatively successful season. I wish there was a few more there to back the players. Let's see what the turnout is like at the next Saturday home game.

But before that, Stratford Town away, and one of the culinary highlights of the season – the legendary Barry's burgers.

Saturday 25 January 2025, Stratford Town FC Vs Halesowen Town FC - Southern League Premier Central

……. and Barry's burger turned out to be the high point of the visit to Knights Lane, in what was a frustrating afternoon of football.

The day had all started well enough. Firstly, I found out that there is a small bus that goes directly from by my house to Rowley Regis train station. From there, it was a pleasant 1 hour 15-minute train ride for Kenny and me, directly to Stratford-upon-Avon.

We met Kev and Sid at the Stratford Alehouse micropub, which I can only describe as banging. Not normally a phrase you would associate with a real ale establishment populated by middle-aged people on a Saturday lunchtime. But there was an excellent DJ, of a certain vintage, spinning classic vinyl tunes from the 60's, 70's, and 80's. The music was completely to the taste of the clientele in the bar, including yours truly. If we did not have a match to go to, we'd have happily whiled away the afternoon there.

Knights Lane is a couple of miles out of Stratford, in Tiddington. So, after a short taxi ride, it was through the turnstiles, where I got a £4 discount with my Blue Light card, and straight to the food stall for one of Barry's Burgers.

I have visited football grounds up and down the country over many decades, and Barry's Burgers are quite simply the best in English football - no others come anywhere close. There is only one word for them – gourmet.

And the amazing thing is, they are incredibly reasonably priced. £3.70 for standard, £3.80 with cheese. Kenny went for £5.10 for double burger and double cheese, and I dined on the bacon and cheeseburger for a meagre £3.90. So, after my Blue Light discount, I still had 10p in my pocket.

Sadly, the quality of Yeltz's football did not match Barry's burgers. Things started badly when less than 10 minutes in Stratford took the lead. Owen James tapped the ball in, after it landed to him. We had some spells of decent passing movements in the first half. But in truth we never properly threatened their goal. At times we played into the hands of their tall and physical back line, by lofting the ball in the air.

They extended their lead to 2-0 on the hour through Kevin Joshua, after a scramble in the box. We huffed and puffed after that, without any real cutting edge, and the full-time score ended that way.

Luckily, most of the teams around us fell to defeats too, so all was not lost, and we remain 3rd. But Kettering and Telford, who are immediately below us, have games in hand. As for our bitter rivals Stourbridge, they lie in 10th, 7 points behind us.

It feels like KD could do with some help up front. His goals have dried up a little, and we have played with one striker in the last couple of games. Despite him being one of the most hardest working forwards at this level, it is tough going for him. A more physical foil is maybe needed. Forward Alex Cameron, who came in from Redditch, has yet to score, but has been on the bench recently. And Charlie Wragg, on short term loan from Walsall, has spent most of the time injured.

After the game the noises on social media were overall predictably quite negative. It is amazing how binary they can be – we win, and people are generally gushing with praise, lose and criticism follows, some of it unreasonable. I know football is an emotive game, and it can be hard to take a step back and look at the bigger picture.

But the bigger picture is that with 15 games to go, there are only 2 teams above us in the league, and we are very much in the hunt for promotion. This defeat comes off the back of 2 weeks where we had midweek fixtures, and that is not to be discounted, especially when we have a small squad. I certainly agree with Russ Penn's post-match comment: "We need to move on quick, the league this season seems to be one of those where anyone can win it, so there is still a long way to go."

The train journey home could have been a grim one. But two fellow Yeltz fans, Steve and Ross, who shared a carriage with us, made it their business to brighten up the journey. We had never met them before, but by the time we got to Rowley Regis station we had talked and laughed about love, life, and the universe, and the defeat was forgotten.

As Kenny and I walked from the station to Fixed Wheel brewery tap to meet Lisa, we both mused that, overall, we'd had a good day. Banging tunes, burgers, and new friends had seen to that. Sometimes on a Saturday, you can have a good time and be in decent spirits despite the football.

February

Saturday 1 February 2025, Halesowen Town FC Vs Bishop's Stortford - Southern League Premier Central

A person wearing a virtual reality headset was on the TV this week, and Lisa was rather impressed with it. She asked Kenny how much they cost, and he gave a one-word answer: "Expensive." I was intrigued why Lisa, a middle-aged woman not prone to liking technological gadgets, was interested. "They'd go down well with the kids at my creches."

Lisa runs her own business, where she supplies creches for corporate events and the like. I said that young children do not need pricey virtual reality headsets. They are easily entertained by traditional games such as dominoes, darts, cards, bingo, carpet bowls, draughts.....I then had to stop myself mid-sentence, because I realised I was subconsciously recreating a social club from the 1970s. Luckily, I cut myself off before suggesting installing hand pulls for bitter and mild, putting ashtrays on the tables, and employing strippers.

Today it was very much actual reality for the Yeltz, and the challenge of Bishop's Stortford. Although the visitors were 8 points were behind us before kick-off, they'd been in fine form recently, and won 4-0 last week. So, on paper this seemed like a game that would be no push over. And paper was the theme of my morning. My mate Phil from London visited to pick up the remaining bounty of his Yeltz programmes.

This time, instead of lugging a suitcase on the train, Phil sensibly arrived by car, with his lovely wife Kat. She understandably questioned, with some jocular prompting from me, why he would want to clog up their London flat with more football programmes. Phil defended himself with a thinly veiled argument that he was trying to preserve an important archive of Yeltz documents. He said he would work with Halesowen Town FC historian Ben Bullock to scan and catalogue them. It was unclear whether Ben knows about this. Kat rolled her eyes, and I giggled. But I guess we all love the eccentric English tradition of collecting things – as long as it's not being done by someone you live with.

Despite Bishop's Stortford's paper threat, the game turned out to be all Yeltz. Well, Yeltz, Yeltz, Yeltz, Yeltz, to be more precise, as we comprehensively beat them 4-0. Other than missing a penalty just before half-time, which Platt admirably saved at 2-0, the visitors barely threatened our goal. And we could have won by a lot more. We were rampant.

Kieren Donnelly terrorised the Bishop's Stortford defence and made them look ragged. Yeltz quickly realised that the tactics did not need to be complicated – get it up to KD and he'll do the rest. And that was the way it was for the first 2 goals, with our top scorer ending his 8-game barren spell, scoring his 18th and 19th of the season in fine fashion.

After the break, right back Jak Hickman did what he does best and delivered a magnificent cross from the byline. Centre half Ryan Wollacott out muscled his marker and planted a textbook header low across Elliot Krasniqi in goal to make it 3-0.

With 20 minutes left McKauley Manning got back to goalscoring ways, when his shot deflected off the defender into the net. Goalkeeper Krasniqi was by far their best player on the day, and if it had not been for him the winning margin would have been greater. It was a thrilling afternoon in front of a better attendance of 1,147 at the Grove.

As we always do, win, lose, or draw, Kenny and I clapped the players, manager and coaching staff in front of us, as they applauded the crowd. KD and Chairman Keith McKenna warmly embraced, and there were beaming smiles all round. Except from one man.

Alex Cameron professionally applauded the fans with all the other players, but he probably had mixed feelings about the day. The striker signed from Redditch over the festive season, no doubt with high hopes about becoming the Yeltz's star man. But in the last couple of games, he has found himself out of the team. And today he was not even on the bench.

A tough situation for the young man, and I felt for him. Football can be a game of a myriad of emotions. In that moment, I could feel the elation of victory wrapped up with empathy for Cameron's predicament. There is only one way back for him - to get his head down and work hard, and when his chance comes, take it.

Some of the results of other teams at the top were in our favour, but the biggest blow came at Sudbury. They were holding Kettering to 0-0 until the 97th minute, before the visitors scored a sickening winner with virtually the last kick of the game.

The Yeltz win has not only boosted our goal difference, but leaves us 4th, a point off top team Telford, with the same number of games played, 28. But Kettering immediately below us have 3 games in hand and are 2 points behind us. We play them away at the end of the month.

After a Yeltz game there are 3 things that I always look forward to: the game highlights and manager's post-match interview on Yeltz TV, and Ben Ditchfield's wonderful match report on the HTFC website. I watched the former two with glee. But this time I could not face the match report.

Our admin at work is off, and my manager has asked me to deal with a whole lot of pressing statistics on Monday. This is not something I like, am good at, or normally do as part of my job. And for the whole weekend it has been filling me with dread. In his match reports Ben likes a stat or two, so I would just find it too triggering to read. So, I decided to give it a skip this week.

A clever person once said, "There are 3 kinds of lies: lies, damned lies, and statistics." I say, there are 3 kinds of work, enjoyable work, unenjoyable work, and f***ing statistics. So, I cannot wait to get this stats task out of the way, so I can once more read Ben Ditchfield's wonderful match reports.

Saturday 8 February 2025, Spalding United Vs Halesowen Town FC - Southern League Premier Central

All I had to go on to piece this one together was Ben Ditchfield's match report, the highlights, and the gaffer's post-match interview. That's because I did not travel the fair old distance to Spalding to witness what was by all accounts a relatively miserable 2-0 defeat.

Newty declared today to be his birthday day out. At 58, he said he might not have many left, so we had better make the most of it. So Newty, Kenny, and I kept it local and went to Aggborough to watch a less miserable defeat, Kidderminster Harriers 1 Chorley 2, in a fairly entertaining top 5 clash.

As ever, football is full of surprises, and just when you think you've seen it all, something new turns up. In this game, it was in the guise of the veteran Kiddy centre-half Paul Downing doing something I've never seen before – a sliding chest. The ball broke and bounced up, and it was just out of Downing's reach. So, he slid and, under pressure from a Chorley player, chested it to teammate Reiss McNally. Something reasonably simple, and effective, but rarely seen.

The Yeltz defeat highlighted two reoccurring themes this season. Firstly, our difficulty in getting any points away from home from teams at the top end of the table – Royston, Bedford, Telford, Stratford, and now Spalding. And secondly, our habit of conceding poor goals.

Spalding's first goal, through Bartosz Cybulski, was the product of Jak Hickman failing to clear. And their second, scored by Sano Sani, followed scrappy Yeltz play. Our home form might be enough to get us into the play-offs. Might. But consistent away form between now and the end of the season is needed, if we want to take that precious top spot and go up automatically.

The defeat means we now fall to 5th, occupying the last play-off spot. And although we have a game in hand, or in some cases 2, on teams above us, Leiston in 6th are now hot on our heels. Next week we have Alvechurch at home, whose form is much improved since ex-Premier League winning goalkeeper Tim Flowers took over as manager. The following Saturday it's the number 9 derby at The Grove. So, a big fortnight, and like the video game of the same name, it is likely to be a battle royale.

If Yeltz have things to reflect on, then I knew after the weekend, I had some contemplation of my own to do. Over the years Newty and I have had many football, and other, days out where we had a few beers during the the day, without much issue. But now, spring chickens we are not. And in my case, I have the added complication of a neurological condition that leaves me wobbly, to one degree or another, most of the time. Even without alcohol. And the serious medication I take to counter the illness has a sedative effect, which is not wholly conducive to our beer drinking habits.

It's also unhelpful that we usually largely forgo the inconvenience of eating during these days on the beer. After lining his stomach before coming out, Newty tends not to eat until his breakfast the following day. But in my case, I opt for the tactic of deferred gratification, kidding myself that I will savour my late-night Chinese take away or pizza. The reality is I eat it like a pack of wild wolves, barely knowing that I have consumed it. So, having something to eat earlier in the day to soak up the beer would be a much more sensible option.

Anyway, Old Father Time tapped me on the shoulder at the end of this particular day out because I was more wobbly than usual. They say old habits die hard. But they also say repeating the same mistakes over is a sign of madness. So, it's down to me to change my habits as I age. Life catches up with you, whether you like it or not.

My football enjoyment this weekend came from Aston Villa beating Spurs 2-1 in the FA Cup 4th round at Villa Park. We've drawn struggling Championship side Cardiff at home in the 5th round. So, with a lot of the big Premier League sides already out of the competition, I am foolishly beginning to think it might finally be our year. They say there is no fool like an old fool. That said, Kenny is caught up with cup fever too. Maybe, it should be there's no fool like a football fan?

Saturday 15 February 2025, Halesowen Town FC Vs Alvechurch FC - Southern League Premier Central

Both the Yeltz and Villa are at home this Saturday and the following one. So, Kenny and I decided to go to one Yeltz game and one Villa. It seemed a fair split of our allegiances. But no coin toss was needed for which games we picked. That's because next Saturday is the

Yeltz Vs Stourbridge number 9 derby, which we are not going to miss for the world.

So, it was off to Villa Park this week, for the game against Ipswich. Which sadly meant missing Yeltz's crucial match against local Worcestershire rivals Alvechurch. But a more sensible example of deferred gratification.

The feeling before this game was this was one that Yeltz really had to win. With 13 games to go in the regular season, our home form is crucial, as we have not always been at our best on our travels. But Alvechurch's mid-table position was misleading, as their recent form was strong, dragging them up the table from their flirtation with the relegation spots.

When the referee signalled half time at Villa Park, an anxious check of social media, for an update of events at the Grove, produced a welcome comfort blanket - which was much needed in the freezing conditions. Yeltz were 2-0 to the good, with goals provided through, who else, but KD, his 20th of season, and the ever-reliable winger Conor Tee, notching his 11th.

All seemed to be going swimmingly at the Grove. More than can be said than at Villa Park. Villa were a little edgy against an Ipswich side who were fighting for their lives in the Premier League. They went in at the break 0-0, though the visitors were reduced to 10 men on 40 minutes. Ipswich then had the temerity to take the lead after the break, through Liam Delap. Although Villa later equalised through Ollie Watkins, they could not finish the job off to claim 3 points.

Leaving Villa Park deflated, Kenny and I at least thought the Yeltz would surely lift our spirits by romping to victory. But it was with disbelief that we discovered that by full-time Alvechurch had managed to level the score at 2-2. What had gone on at the Grove? Well, Facebook quickly provided one of the answers to that question. Not long after half time skipper Ryan Wynter was shown a straight red card, after bringing down an Alvechurch player, who was through on goal. We would have to wait until later to discover more details.

The details bought a sense of disbelief. It looked like we were all over Alvechurch in the first 45 minutes and could have had a bigger lead than 2-0. Our normally reliable keeper Platty made a bit of a hash of their first goal, which allowed them back into the game. Wynter was sent off at 2-1, but oddly there was no footage on the highlights. One fan, who sat in line with the incident, posted on social media that the Alvechurch player was offside.

On the hour our nemesis struck again - conceding from corners. This time, ex-Kidderminster Harriers defender Krystian Pearce headed in directly from the kick. But even then, we should have won it - after some good work KD found himself 10 yards out, middle of the goal, with the ball on his right foot, the goal gaping, and only the keeper to beat. But his shot hit the bar and bounced down the wrong side of the line. It was not to be our day.

In his post-match interview, gaffer Russ Penn summed up KD, who earlier in the game scored a magnificent glancing header: "He scores the goals that he has no right to score, then he misses the chances that he's got to score."

If KD did score the simpler chances, he'd probably have scored 35 goals this campaign by now. But even so, as of today, he is the league's leading marksman anyway. Regardless, us Yeltzfolk absolutely love him. He's not the biggest, but every game he knocks around far larger defenders, and he does not stop running for the cause.

Drawing the game from a winning position did not only lower the mood a little, but it also lowered our league position. We are now outside of the playoff spots for the first time in a long while. We are in 6th, on 50 points, having played 30 matches. But leaders Bedford are on 56 having played 2 games more, and Telford in 2nd on 55 having played one game more. So, it is still incredibly tight, in what has been a topsy turvy title and promotion race.

It is still all to play for, and a win against our bitter rivals Stourbridge next week could see us healthily back in the playoff mix. At this stage of the season, with our promotion aspirations, the fixture takes on more importance than usual, if that is possible.

Walking back to the car from Villa Park my brother Warwick asked how the Yeltz had got on. He does take a passing interest in the results, given my passion for the club. He asked if the club should have done better in their recent history, given they are generally better supported that most other teams in the league.

I found myself on the defensive a little, trying to justify some of the reasons for why the Yeltz are still at non-League step 3. And there are good reasons, some to do with previous ownership. But now feels like the right time for the club to finally progress to the next level. But it is not easy. For every Halesowen Town FC, there are handful of other clubs in the league realistically competing for the same outcome. And there are only 2 treasured promotion spots - one automatic, and one through the play-offs. So, squeezing your way up through the bottleneck at the top of the league usually boils down to the finest of margins.

As the number of games left decreases, the tension proportionately increases. It starts to become less about who can play the best football, and more about who can more competently hold their nerve.

I regularly see a chiropractor named Harish, a friendly Liverpool fan. This is because of enduring problems with my neck, back, and shoulders. But at the moment I might be wasting my money seeing him. Because what might really be causing the problems to those bodily parts is the weight of expectation of getting promoted.

Saturday 22 February 2025, Halesowen Town FC Vs Stourbridge FC - Southern League Premier Central

The feeling before this one was that it was a question of resilience, toughness, survival almost, and one either way could make the difference. The new tactics needed to work. I'm not talking about the game, but my day out on the beer with Newty. You'll remember after our last day out together I ended more wobbly than normal. So, today I was determined to be more sensible.

Newty, Kenny, and I went to Wetherspoons at lunchtime. It started well. I had lunch. Hell, even Newty had lunch. I accompanied my lunch with blackcurrant squash. You read that correct. You do not need to clean your glasses. It was horrible. The squash in and of itself was not horrible - I drink gallons of blackcurrant squash at home - it was just horrible not drinking beer. But then for the first time this year, I had a sudden brainwave.

A few weeks before Christmas I remember being in Wetherspoons at lunchtime and not wanting a drink. So, I ordered an Erdinger Alkoholfrei Beer and found it to be good – so I had one of those. And that got me through until it was time to leave for the match. I'd done it. On a day out with Newty and Kenny I was stone cold sober after the pre-match drink. My reward? Unprecedented queues to get in at the Grove, backing up way down Old Hawne Lane, despite us arriving in good time before kick-off.

The long queue to get in was problematic, because the symptoms of my neurological condition were quite severe. So, standing in the queue was quite challenging. And in all honesty, my illness was part of the reason I stayed sober before the game.

By the time we arrived at the turnstiles, we could hear the referee's whistle signalling the start of the game. Not too bad we thought - within seconds we would be on the East Terrace watching the action. But then there was a sound we did not want to hear – a sudden cheer. But a cheer not loud enough to signal that Yeltz had scored, meaning that Stourbridge had. Less than a minute gone, and we were 1-0 down. It transpired a long ball over the top was not dealt with by the defence or keeper Platty, and striker Ethan Freemantle nipped in to slot home.

Once we forced our way through the full house crowd to somewhere near our normal spot on the East Terrace, a couple of things were evident. Firstly, it was an absolutely resplendent scene for the oldest continuously played derby in the West Midlands. Not only were the fans crammed into the Grove from both towns in good spirits, but the famous old ground was bathed in radiant sunshine. Secondly, even though there were only a few minutes on the clock, the pitch was starting to cut up badly. This would make it hard for us to pass the ball around, favouring Stourbridge.

The first half went how you would expect a local derby to go on a cut up pitch. It was scrappy. Stourbridge dug trenches and defended their lead well. We were limited to few chances, the most notable of which fell to KD, 6 yards out. But at the critical moment he slipped, and the opportunity was lost. A frustrating first half saw us trail 0-1 at the break.

Largely, the second half was more of the same. Our bitter rivals seemed content to hold onto their lead and not venture forward a great deal. But we were struggling to break them down and get into any kind of rhythm. Wide men Mini Macca and Conor Tee could not find the right keys to unlock the door, and Stourbridge's rugged back 3 were marshalling KD well. I was beginning to develop a sense of great dread that we were not going to score, and it was not going to be our day. That is a bad enough feeling to have in any game, but on derby day it can make you sick to the stomach.

70 minutes were on the clock. Around this time, in this situation, some managers would give it the 'we'll give it 5 more minutes and see what happens' treatment. Such hesitation or indecision can be costly. Not Russ Penn. When action needs to be taken, he's decisive. He replaced Reece Mitchell and Macca with Ben Cassidy and Milan Butterfield, then 2 minutes later Reece Flanagan with striker Charlie Wragg. All 3 substitutes had a big impact.

I said to Kenny, "Wragg has yet to score for us, and I can just feel that this is his moment." Immediately Cassidy and Butterfield made a difference, the former with bursting runs down the left, and the latter with his physical presence. We started to build pressure and momentum. Then on 79 minutes my prophetic words came to pass. Following a Yeltz corner, flicked on by Wollacott, the ball landed to Wragg. He wriggled a yard of space and fired a shot through legs that found its way into the back of the net.

The sickness in my stomach made way for pure, unmitigated joy. I found myself jumping up and down on my least bag leg screaming, "Get in, get f*cking in!" about a dozen times on a loop. When I finally calmed down, I realised that the crowd around me had settled down from the goal long before I had. I did not care one jot. We had equalised, that was all that mattered.

Now I could smell blood. There was only going to be one winner in this game, and it was not going to be Stourbridge. And another thing was for sure, there was no way that KD was going to leave this pitch without a goal. You could sense it coming.

We carried on battering on the door, driven on by the fevered Yeltz crowd, and come it did. With 5 minutes to go, Conor Tee floated in a delicious inswinging free kick from 30 yards out. Milan Butterfield made it his, heading into the dangerous area between the sticks. You can guess the rest. An unmarked, and onside KD was there to triumphantly slam it into the Stourbridge net. 2-1 to the Yeltz, and a turnaround that at one point I really could not see coming. Which made it all the sweeter.

But the game was not over, and inevitably Stourbridge pushed for the equaliser. This is when, in an anxious frenzy, you shout at everybody and anybody, most of it irrational and aimed at the officials. And do things like cheer offsides, throw ins, and goal kicks that go in your favour.

But deep into injury time, just when I thought I could not bear it anymore, Wollacott headed clear to Charlie Wragg on the right wing. He dribbled and finally slid in a ball behind the visitor's defence, sending KD clear. Our star striker finished with aplomb, slotting home his 22nd goal of the season. It was over. We had won. And we had retained the Brookes-Clark Charity Shield, for the overall winners of the 2 derby games in the season.

I was on cloud number 9. To win is one thing, but to have gone so long in the game thinking we were going to lose, is another. But you cannot doubt this bunch. Because they always come back fighting.

As soon as the final whistle sounded, the misery guts Newty came out with his usual line: "Come on, let's go to the pub." Kenny and I always ignore him, as we stay and clap the players and staff, regardless of the result. But on this occasion, even Newty seemed happy enough to disregard his own comment and give the players the credit they deserved.

One thing was for sure, after this victory I was going to enjoy a pint or two. And we all did just that. But I managed to stay relatively sensible. Finally, at 53, I seem to be making some progress as a grown up.

The win means we now have the best home record in the league so far this season. It's a shame our away record is not so impressive, or we would be in for a better shout of the top spot and automatic promotion. As it stands, we are 5th, and the play-offs is probably the best we can hope for, unless we have a good run of form and other teams trail off. The defeat for Stourbridge condemns them to 10th, 8 points behind us. And crushes any realistic hopes they had of making the play-offs.

We dashed to the comforting arms of the Coombs Wood Sports and Social Club for a welcoming pint and cob, to watch Villa Vs Chelsea in the 5.30 kick off on TV. The club, which Kenny and I have been members of for many years, bucks the general trend in the decline of contemporary social clubs. It is busy and bustling with both young and older punters. They all enjoy the well-appointed, and recently refurbished, indoor surroundings, which open out onto the patio and cricket pitch, overlooking the countryside beyond.

The key to the club's ongoing success, under Dawn and her committee, seems to be that, unlike many other clubs, the client base is not concentrated around people of a certain age. Here families, children, and younger people mix with people of older vintage. And as long as the next generation of members continues to come through, the longevity of the club will hopefully be secured.

I only started frequenting the club in my 30's, when it was in a different location. But when Lisa, Kenny, and I went to the last bonfire night celebration at the club, it struck me that it has been a part of the whole of Kenny's life. And that for him, throughout his childhood and now into his early adult years, it's always been a place of warmth and happiness. Somewhere that's always been there for him. I guess there are similarities with me and the Grove. And what a fitting day to celebrate both those wonderful places.

Tuesday 25 February 2025, Kettering Town Vs Halesowen Town FC - Southern League Premier Central

The week started with this statement from the club: "Halesowen Town Football Club can confirm that Adi Yussuf has had his contract cancelled by mutual consent. We wish Adi all the best for the future."

Any Yeltz fan who shed a tear over this news, would be a very odd creature indeed. Yussuf – or Adi Useless as he came to be known - came to the Grove in close season in the blaze of publicity on a reputedly decent contract.

His reputation was that he had been capped 4 times by Tanzania and had a Football League and higher non-League pedigree. There were high hopes for the striker. But he looked sluggish and unfit in pre-season, and things never really improved from there.

Now, a handful of appearances, and an equal number of goals and red cards later – one - and he has finally gone. The saying goes, you take a risk with every player you sign. To be fair to Russ Penn, his recruitment record is very good. But Yussuf is one to be forgotten.

A contract though has two parties to it. The club fulfilled its obligation by paying the player. It could be argued that Yussuf never properly fulfilled his, by not doing enough to force his way into the team and only scoring one goal during his stay. You can lead a horse to water, but you can't make it drink.

My start to the week also saw me undertaking a familiar ritual – watching Kidderminster Harriers highlights of their game on Saturday, and gaffer Phil Brown's post-match interview, while on my exercise bike at lunchtime. This is generally pleasant, regardless of Kiddy's result, as it distracts me from being out of breath on my bike sprints.

But this Monday, Brown's chat with interviewer Matty Paddock was pretty dark after their 3-1 home defeat to Spennymoor Town, which capped recent poor form. I enjoy trips to Aggborough, am fond of Harriers, and hope that Brown can lead the club back to the National

League. So, at times this interview with the gaffer was hard to watch. Amongst the things he said were:

"The players out there today wore the shirt with no pride whatsoever."

"There was no ambition to win the game, at times they were going through the motions, and that is a representation of me."

"There's something going on in the changing rooms and I don't know what it is….. it's almost like they didn't want me at the football club ….. if that's the case, I'd love one of them to step up in front of the cameras and say them words."

Brown went on to apologise to the fans and say he's told the players that they will be training on Sunday. Watching the interview, I could not help but feel for Brown. Having the feeling of being let down by your players as a manager or coach is not pleasant. Ultimately, as the person in charge, once the players cross that white line, you have a lack of control, and you must trust your charges. But when that trust is not repaid, you can feel disrespected and betrayed.

Fortunately, Russ Penn did not have to say sorry to the Yeltz faithful who travelled to Latimer Park to watch this top of the table clash. I did not go, as Villa were away at Crystal Palace on TV, and my light wallet told me that was the better option. Penn started with the same 11 who finished the game against Stourbridge on Saturday with a flourish. He rewarded all 3 of Cassidy, Butterfield, and Wragg for impactful contributions from the bench. Jamie Willets, on dual registration with

Tamworth, continued to deputise for the suspended skipper Ryan Wynter.

Yeltz left Kettering with a valuable point, after a rare but well-earned clean sheet, in a 0-0 draw. From the jigsaw I put together from Halesowen Town Radio, Yeltz TV highlights, and the boss's post-match interview, it was a keenly contested match that we had the better of. The best chances of the game fell to KD and Butterfield, and we might have snatched it.

Russ Penn: "I thought we were outstanding. I cannot believe we did not win the game at the end; I think their keeper won man of the match, which sums it up. Full credit to Kettering, it was a good game, but we were on the front foot throughout."

This season we have had a habit of conceding silly goals. So, this clean sheet on the road at one of the title favourites, might do us as much good as if we had won but conceded. And on the back of the morale boosting victory over Stourbridge, and with the squad in good nick, it feels like we are in a good position for the final push of the season.

In his post-match interview on Yeltz TV, in reply to a question by interviewer Frank Williams about teams in the top 5 having played a different number of games, Penn wisely said: "I try not to take any notice of anybody else, because then I take my eyes off us and we've got 30 points to play for. And if we get those 30 points we will be right up there."

Penn, his staff, and his squad seem determined and focused. Looking at the fixtures, other teams in the top

6 have tougher run-ins than us. We remain 5th but looking at permutations like games in hands and teams we have to play, we are not yet entirely out of the running for the top spot. It is still all to play for with 10 games to go.

But we all know things can change quickly in football, so that determination and focus needs to be steadfast. Take Kidderminster Harriers and Phil Brown, for example.   Tonight, they overcame Kings Lynn 2-0 at Aggborough. Brown seemed altogether more upbeat in his interview, and things are rosier in the garden. All in the space of 3 days. To quote another classic football cliché, a win can change everything.

March

Saturday 1 March 2025, Biggleswade Town FC Vs Halesowen Town FC Vs - Southern League Premier Central

There was bad news in the week with the news of the passing of BBC Hereford & Worcester's Steve Miller, who was a long-time commentator on Kidderminster Harriers games. I listened to Steve's distinctive commentaries, while catching up on Kiddy's weekend game highlights, during my Monday lunchtime exercise bike sessions.

The familiarity of Steve's voice and style was comforting. I did not realise how much so, until I heard about his death, which saddened me a great deal. I did not even know he was ill, as he was working up until recently. He will be sorely missed.

Villa's FA Cup 5th round tie against championship side Cardiff City was moved to last night, a Friday, 8pm kick-off. This was disappointing because it broke from the tradition of FA Cup games being played at 3 o'clock on a Saturday. But more so, because I find night games an increasing struggle to cope with these days, due to my neurological condition. Because as the day way wears on, I get increasingly fatigued, dizzy, and lightheaded, amongst other things.

It is a battle to stand up on the Holte End for the length of the match. I have strong sensations that I'm going to fall over. My legs feel week, and my head swims. I only stay upright with the help of my walking stick and sheer determination. And I cannot sit down, because everyone by us stands, so I would not be able to see the action on the pitch. Evening games are as much of a test of endurance, as they are enjoyment. I watch the minutes passing by on the scoreboard and think to myself things like, "Come on Dom, you can do this. Only 10 minutes to half time, then you can have a sit down."

For next season, I could look to swap mine and Kenny's season ticket seats to a more conducive location, where I could sit down. But we have stood in the same spot with the same people for many years, and it would significantly diminish our matchday experience if we moved. And Kenny is able bodied, and it seems grossly unfair on him to suffer because of my frailties. So, for now at least, I think I'll just soldier on and see how it goes.

Regarding today's Yeltz game, on the face of it, the sensible view would be that victory should be assured. Before kick-off Biggleswade were rooted to the bottom of the league, more than 10 points adrift of the next placed team, Hitchin. But their recent form was not bad, showing that they are no pushovers.

With Biggleswade being a fair trip, and my health currently not being great, Kenny and I gave this one a skip. But with Villa having already played, and Kiddy unusually playing on Sunday, we had to find a game to go to. After scouring the non-League fixture lists, we settled on Bromsgrove Sporting Vs Sudbury. Firstly, because we are both fond of the Victoria Ground, and, secondly, there was something on the game, as both needed the points at the bottom end of the table.

Our view that the Victoria Ground is a lovely setting to watch football might be coloured by the fact that every time we go, there is warm sunshine. But even if the weather was cold or wet, I think it would be a pleasant setting, nonetheless.

Before kick-off we did 2 routine things - checked the Yeltz team lineup on social media and migrated towards the food outlet. The Yeltz were unchanged from the Kettering game. At the food hut, those who ordered burgers were being handed a numbered chitty and had to wait. With kick-off drawing near, Kenny suggested we deviate from our normal pre-match cheeseburgers, and instead opt for hot Cornish pasties, as they were ready to serve. I agreed, and it turned out to be a wise suggestion from the young man. Not only did the pasties make a pleasant change but they were delicious too. Literally food for thought for future football cuisine choices.

We stood in the sun eating our tasty pasties and admiring the wonderful skills, passing, and attacking attributes of Bromsgrove's brilliant Jamie Meddows. He provided superb entertainment. I looked across at Kenny and thought how incredibly lucky I am to have such an amazing son. He is happy to spend his Saturday afternoons with his old Dad, us together indulging our shared passion of football. The next day, when we were alone, I told him I loved him, and I was very proud of him. I am sure he knows these things anyway, but it does not cost anything to say them.

Bromsgrove, who had dominated the first 45 minutes, extended their lead to 2-0 over a labouring Sudbury, with literally the last kick of the half. The marvellous

Meddows scored both. As the referee blew his whistle, our thoughts quickly turned to Yeltz. I was expecting a half-time lead. But it turned out to be an anticlimax: 0-0. Oh well, we philosophised. It's never easy on the road, and there is still a long way to go.

Kenny and I do not usually look at our phones for score updates when we are watching a game, as this tends to detract from watching. But with Bromsgrove comfortably in control, and us getting increasingly anxious about the events at Langford Road, Biggleswade, we could not help ourselves. 70 minutes, still 0-0. What was going on down there? Had we missed a boat load of chances? Was their keeper having a blinder? Were we having an off day? One thing was for sure; we desperately needed a goal.

Trouble is, I had broken the golden rule of not looking at my phone, and in a state of heightened tension, I could not help myself, and I started to look every few minutes. And as time ticked on, still no Yeltz goal. On 85 minutes Bromsgrove's Theo Robinson smartly lobbed the Sudbury keeper to put the game to bed at 3-0. Yeltz had still not broken the deadlock, and Kenny and I started to feel a little frantic.

As full time blew at the Victoria Ground, our phones were showing 90 minutes in the Yeltz game. But hope remained. These days there is always a fair chunk of stoppage time. As we walked back to Kenny's car, we constantly refreshed our phones, which continued to show an achingly frustrating scoreline of Biggleswade 0 Yeltz 0.

We arrived at Kenny's car, got in, belted up, and knew by then the game was up. A no goals draw. Ok, a point on the road and another clean sheet. But realistically, we had needed a win against the league's bottom club. I gave my phone one last despairing refresh. AND I COULD NOT BELIEVE IT!!!! BECAUSE IT READ 'Biggleswade Town FC 0 Halesowen Town FC 1'!!!!!

If anyone had been walking past the car at that moment, they must have wondered what was going on. Because we were screaming, banging the dashboard, and generally going wild. And whether there was anybody walking past or not, I genuinely cannot tell you, as I was lost in that jubilant moment.

It turned out that substitute Alex Cameron scored in the very last minute of normal time, after good work by Mini Macca, to steal the priceless 3 points. Un-believable. And on a personal note for Cameron, I am delighted for him. He has fallen out of favour recently, so it is great for him to have this moment of glory. Sadly, Russ Penn did not witness it, as he was suspended for this one, leaving his trusty assistant Gary Whild in charge in the dugout.

The win leaves us still 5th in the table. But if we win our game in hand on leaders Bedford, we will only be 2 points behind them. Significantly, there is now a 6-point gap between us and 6th placed Stamford, although they do have a game in hand. Remember, the Champions go up automatically, with the next 4 teams going into the play-offs.

With no mid-week game, the players have a whole week to prepare before next Saturday. As we face

Banbury at home, Kenny and I can watch the game in the flesh, meaning we do not have to apprehensively wait for game updates on our phones. After this one, the thing that needs a refresh before next Saturday is me.

Saturday 8 March 2025, Halesowen Town FC Vs Banbury United FC - Southern League Premier Central

Before this game Banbury were 13th in the league, 16 points off the playoffs, and 7 ahead of the relegation zone. With it being the springtime run-in to the season, it posed the classic question: will the visitors be on the beach, or free of pressure and be able to express themselves, and cause the Yeltz problems? But we knew that regardless of Banbury's attitude, if we play to our full potential, we should win.

Personally, my biggest challenge was just getting to the game and lasting the duration. Since last weekend my health has deteriorated, and just walking short distances was proving difficult. Kenny had to drop me as close to the Stourbridge Road turnstiles as possible, and we had to forego our usual spot on the East Terrace for seats in the Harry Rudge Stand. Fortunately, non-League football at this level provides that flexibility. Once you enter the ground, you can choose your vantage point, and whether to stand or sit.

I do not mind sitting in the Harry Rudge Stand, as it gives you a good view of the rest of the ground. And unlike standing on the East Terrace, on a bright day like today, you have not got the sun in your eyes. But like most seating areas in football grounds, the fans are more reserved. So, I feel less inclined to shout, bawl, and cheer, which can lead to a frustrating amount of pent-up emotion during some periods of the game. But I was just grateful that I was just about well enough to attend, though it was a close call. Before kick-off I was feeling pretty awful, and I was thinking about going home. But the obligatory pre-match cheeseburger just about swung it in my favour, and I stayed.

There were some changes to the team. It is not unusual these days for managers to rotate, even if the team won the previous game. But one change seemed like a particularly big call. Centre-half Ryan Wollacott has been a mainstay of the team all season, starting more games than any other player. A solid, no nonsense, reliable defender, who has proved to be a fantastic signing.

In the last 3 games Wollacott has partnered Jamie Willetts, on dual registration with Tamworth. Willetts stepped in to cover skipper Ryan Wynter's absence, following suspension. We won all 3 games, the last 2 keeping clean sheets. Wynter was back from his ban for the trip the Biggleswade last week. But as the Wollacott and Willetts partnership was impressive in his absence, he had to make do with a spot on the bench. But today, Wollacott finds himself sub, with Willetts and Wynter starting.

For all I know, Wollacott might be carrying a knock, or might be recovering from an illness. But on the face of it, it just looks like Russ Penn made what he thought was the right decision for this specific game. Football can be a brutal business. I'm sure Wollacott had no thoughts of being left out today, unless the gaffer pulled him to one side in training on Thursday. Football is, of course, a team game, but at times your heart goes out to individuals.

As the game started it was clear that the roles of the central defenders on both teams were going to be key. That was because the pitch was dry and bumpy, and consequently the ball was in the air a lot. So, aerial dominance was important. The triangular base of Willetts and Wynter, with Butterfield in front of them, overpowered their Banbury counterparts in what was a first half of attrition, but little football. There was only one chance of note, it fell to KD, who shot wide.

At half time I said to Kenny, despite the tricky pitch, we need to get the ball down and play if we want to create the chances to win. Russ Penn must have said the same at half time, because that's what happened in the second half. Our ball players like Parker, Smile, Tee, and Mini Macca started to take control.

But when the goal came, 10 minutes after the break, it was more the product of tenacity and individual brilliance, than intricate passing. KD was put through wide on the left but looked second favourite in a contest of strength with rugged Banbury defender Yaw Ofusu. But as KD so often does, he out-muscled the bigger man. He then cut across the defender and slotting the ball past keeper Jack Harding for his 24th goal of the season. I momentarily lost my seated fan decorum by standing up and frantically fist pumping, shouting, "Get in there KD, you f*cking beauty!!!" It was a goal that deserved at least one expletive.

The effervescent wide man Conor Tee did his level best to make it 2-0, hitting both post and bar with magnificent efforts, but he was not to get his goal. In the end, one goal was enough against a persistent Banbury side, in what was a solid and thoroughly professional performance.

Before the game Russ Penn said at this stage of the season performances do not matter so much, it's the results that count. Absolutely. And this game summed that up perfectly. Was Penn's decision to leave Wollacott out justified? Well, we won and Willetts and Wynter were key men. There's no saying we would not have won with Wollacott in the team. But at times managers must make big decisions. And I would rather they make them than shirk them, as long as they are done honestly and properly. These decisions can be the difference between success and failure. And you must applaud Penn for having the boldness to make the big call.

On viewing the other results, the day got even better. Promotion chasing rivals Kettering lost, Telford drew, and for once we were happy Stourbridge won – because they beat Stratford. This all means we are now 3rd, only 2 points behind leaders Bedford, having played the same games. Kettering are in 2nd, on the same points as us but with a game in hand. Crucially though, their form is stuttering.

So, without getting carried away, and knowing it's best to concentrate on one game at a time, we probably have a better chance of winning the league than any stage this season. I have been through the drama of play-offs before, both ending in promotion and failure.

Going up as Champions would not only be glorious but a blessed relief.

Before the game I felt ill. I still feel ill, but I'm delighted that we won. If only the NHS could provide winning on prescription.

Saturday 15 March 2025, Hitchin Town FC Vs Halesowen Town FC - Southern League Premier Central

Given my recent dreadful health, things turned a little sinister this week with a tailored advertisement that popped up on my Facebook messenger account: "Book your pure cremation now! £100 off introductory offer, ends 31 March." Does this mean I need to be cremated before then? Sadly, I cannot commit at such short notice, because Yeltz's last fixture is not until 26 April, and after that there might be play-off games. Maybe if we get promoted, a barbecue will do instead.

On Wednesday Villa beat Club Brugge at Villa Park to go through to the quarter finals of the Champions League for the first time since 1982. Sadly, I was too unwell to go and had to make do with watching it on TV. The tickets for the next round, against Paris Saint-Germain, are on sale soon, but I am not sure whether I will buy mine. Kenny cannot go, as he will be on holiday in Tenerife, and I'm not sure if I will be well enough to go. So, I do not want to waste £70 on a ticket.

Besides all that, unlike most Villa fans, I have not really felt myself swept up in the wave of excitement that these Champions League games have generated. For me, the main prize I covet for Villa this season is the FA

Cup. We face Preston North End away at the end of the month, and to me that fixture is a lot more alluring. I've never been to Deepdale, but would love to, especially with it being one of the oldest football grounds in the country.

Trying to get tickets for Villa's away games is almost impossible, unless you go to them regularly. But being a season ticket holder and having attended all the FA Cup games so far, I had a chance of getting 2 of the remaining tickets. I logged onto the Aston Villa website at the allocated time, and was excited to see there were tickets left, so I reserved 2. I clicked on 'choose your seats', but it said 'error!' I clicked back, but then it was apparent the tickets were sold out. My Deepdale dream was over.

I was hoping to travel to Hitchin for this Yeltz game. But as I monitored my health during this week, it became increasingly clear that my dream of getting to this game was over too. Going to any game today was too much of a challenge. Just walking a few yards up the road is difficult. So, for the first time in as long as I can remember I spent Saturday afternoon not in the comforting confines of a football stadium. But I did get out of the house to watch football at a venue which is the next best thing – Newty's shed.

A few years ago, before the COVID pandemic, Newty tasked himself with building a garden shed for storage. But once he started the project, he decided he might as well sneak in a bar, with a 60" TV, to watch football. He named it the Dugout.

Since then, Kenny, Newty, and I have watched most major football games in the Dugout: cup finals of all sorts, domestic and European, play-offs, World Cups, European Championships, major international games etc. Not to mention that Newty spends a fair proportion of his life in there watching football, when he is not at work or sleeping, or out with his wife Lou. With me being housebound for a while, just being out was a breath of fresh air. Or to be more correct, stale, farty air.

The information coming from Hitchin's Top Field ground in the first half was that the contest was quite even, with both teams having chances. It sounded like you could not tell which team were pushing for promotion, and who was in the bottom 3. But things changed quickly after the break with Yeltz going 2-0 up within the space of 5 minutes. The scorers were predictable – Conor Tee, and KD, notching their 12th and 25th goals of the season respectively. Yeltz held the lead until 90+4, when Hitchin pulled one back to make it 2-1. But it was too little, too late, and the points were ours.

Next, our eyes turned to our promotion rivals' results: Stratford lost, Kettering and Bedford drew. Even though Telford won, the scores meant an amazing thing – we have gone top of the league. Us, Telford, and Bedford are all on 63 points, but we have a marginally superior goal difference. Only Kettering have a single game in hand now, and not everything there is rosy in the garden.....

At one point it looked like Kettering were going to run away with the league, and they even dumped League 2

Doncaster out of the FA Cup. But since then, things have not been plain sailing, and their form has slowly got worse. This week, Isiah Noel-Williams, who Kettering fans seem to regard as their best player this season, left the club in mysterious circumstances.

Noel-Williams' social media statement hinted that all is not well at the club. After Saturday's game there were some reports of heated disagreements between fans and boss Richard Lavery. All of this could be to Yeltz's advantage. Kettering play their game in hand away at Alvechurch on Tuesday, and hopefully our Worcestershire neighbours can do us a favour.

There were reports from Hitchin of jubilant and raucous singing from the Yeltz fans in the bar after the game. To the extent that the bar staff had to tell them to quieten down, as they could not hear what customers were ordering. This made me extremely jealous that I was not well enough to make the trip.

Russ Penn has rightly repeatedly said he's not distracted by the noise of other team's results. He is just concentrating on the Yeltz and not looking too far into the future. In The Non-League Paper he said: "I know it's as boring as anything, and I'm going to sound like a broken record, but you really can't do anything but focus on your next game."

But with 7 games to go, we are in great form, leading the league, and have a striker who's on fire. As a fan, it's impossible not to get excited. I just hope I am well enough to get down to the Grove next Saturday for the visit of Lowestoft. The Yeltz might be on top of the world right now, but I certainly am not. I just hope this week I turn a corner and start to perk up a bit.

Saturday 22 March 2025, Halesowen Town FC Vs Lowestoft Town - Southern League Premier Central

Like a lot of non-League clubs, Yeltz do a 50/50 draw, with 50% of the takings going to the club, and the remainder to the lucky winner. I have yet to win it, but I live in hope. I jocularly asked the ticket seller this week the same question I always do, "Is this ticket the winner?" The answer was a starkly honest one: "I doe know mate."

But the more worrying 50/50 for this game was whether I was going to be able to attend. Yesterday it was touch and go, as I was very dizzy. But a lie in, and 24 hours further recovery, was fortunately just about sufficient to make me well enough to go to the Grove.

Newty text me to inquire about my health, and to see if I would be fit enough to go to the game. When I have spells of ill health with my neurological condition, I can sense Newty getting overly concerned. The reason for that is we lost two of our close friends when they were in their 40s, and for him I am last man standing. I'm a gateway for him getting out for a few beers and watching football outside of his shed. If I were to die, it would be a disaster for Newty. It would not be too pleasant for me either, if I'm being honest.

On the note of beer, there is an exciting new development at the Grove – a new bar in the Stourbridge Road end. This pleased Newty no end, with it being pretty close to our seats in the Harry

Rudge stand, me still being too frail to stand. With new permanent toilets also added there recently, it feels like the club is gearing up for promotion.

It did not feel like we were gearing up for promotion with 3 minutes on the clock though, as we were 1-0 down. A quality delivery from the right off a free-kick was met with a free header, which hit the post. Lowestoft's Kyle Haylock was first to follow up, to slot home. This led to a feeling of dread that it might not be our day. Conceding an early goal does not normally lead me to such gloomy thoughts, but it compounded the fact that top scorer Kieren Donnelly was missing, a victim of flu. Other players were absent too, and some had to play despite still not being fully recovered.

With KD and fellow striker Charlie Wragg being out ill, it was a rare chance for Alex Cameron to start. Sometimes opportunity knocks in football when you least expect it, and it is up to you to grasp the chance with both hands. It was now up to Cameron to prove he was up to the occasion. And from the first whistle the young man signalled that he was. He won headers, competed well, and held the ball up when needed. The number 9 felt light, not heavy on his back.

Lowestoft keeper Ronnie Yeo only looked like a teenager, and he is not the biggest either. So, Yeltz sensibly launched the ball into the box at every opportunity. But credit to Yeo, he generally dealt with things well. Then on the half hour chaos in the visitor's box led to Yeltz skipper Ryan Wynter belting it in from 6 yards. 1-1.

A mere 4 mins later Conor Tee took a free kick, and Yeltz won several contacts, before the ball was slammed in on the volley at close range by Alex Cameron. 2-1. I was delighted for Cameron, and it was no more than he deserved. Once we were in front, a youthful and relegation threatened Lowestoft side looked demoralised. They had that, 'here we go again' look about them.

Just before the break a Yeltz corner was not cleared, and the ball landed to the mercurial left foot of Mini Macca, 12 yards out. It felt like there was only going to be one outcome, and it came to pass. Macca smashed his shot low into the back of the net, followed by his trademark acrobatic double somersault celebration. It made me even more dizzy just watching him. 3-1, and even though there was another half of football to go, Lowestoft looked beaten.

We had plenty of pressure and chances in the second half, but the score remained 3-1. It is easy to think that we should have scored more to extend our goal difference. But equally we did not concede to make it a nervy 3-2. And let's remember we had a flu-riddled team. And all in front of a bumper crowd of 1,584 on what is Non-League Day.

Kettering and Telford drew, so despite others winning, we are top of the league by the slender margin of 2 goals, ahead of Bedford. There are now just 6 games remaining. It feels equally thrilling and excruciating. We just need to keep winning. There are 2 routes to promotion - the title or the play-offs. One route is certain and paved with glory. The other is treacherous, where success is more of a relief.

I'm absolutely overjoyed. Not only that we won, and are league leaders, but that I got to the game. I always have a little moment during the game when I just take a breath, look around the ground, take in the atmosphere and the occasion, and think to myself how lucky I am to be there. When I'm with Kenny, I watch him engrossed in the game, just for a second or two, and feel how much I love him. I do this every game. But today it felt extra special, as it was a triumph just being inside a football ground on Saturday afternoon. My rightful place.

Saturday 29 March 2025, Harborough Town Vs Halesowen Town FC - Southern League Premier Central

This week, there was good news and bad prior to this game. The good news is that my health has started to improve. To the extent that by Friday, when I walked down the street, instead of feeling like a frail, dizzy, 90-year-old man, I felt like a frail, dizzy, 80-year-old man. And after my Saturday lie in, I had progressed to the sprightly standard of a frail, dizzy, 70-year-old man. That was enough to see me on the way to Harborough with Kenny to watch this top of the table clash, with the home side being 5th place in the league.

The bad news is that while us Yeltzfolk are enjoying an exciting promotion race, our fiercest rivals, Stourbridge FC, are concerned about their very future. They posted a statement on social media saying that some of their stands, and some floodlights, at their War Memorial Ground, are unsafe. That's because they are too close to grass banks behind the stands, damaged by builders. The unsafe stands and floodlights will be dismantled after the last game of the season. It appears that currently the club are unsure if they will be able to play at the War Memorial Ground next season. And if not, what ground they will use for home matches.

Even though the Glassboys are our bitter rivals, I feel for their plight, and I hope the club can resolve the situation soon. I also hope they can continue to play at the War Memorial Ground, because it can be a slippery slope moving away from your home. Other Midlands teams like Dudley Town and Worcester City, have found this, for different reasons. And of course, we want to keep our 145-year-old local derby going. Although all Yeltzfolk hope we will be in the division above next season.

Harborough Town's Beehive ground is a neat and tidy new build stadium with a gleaming 4G astroturf surface, and swish facilities. The Beehive is a great set-up, and progress is of course inevitable, with teams moving to new stadiums for good reasons. But I much prefer the historic and characterful Grove, and I hope we always remain there and play on the only true footballing surface of grass.

We were delighted to see that KD was back in the starting lineup. This was at the expense of Alex Cameron. Also, Jamie Willets once again replaced Ryan Wollacott. Both Cameron and Wollacott had played extremely well in last week's win, so it shows that the manager is prepared to be ruthless in this pursuit of promotion.

With me still being doddery, Kenny and I took seats in the stand. One of the difficulties of sitting down at a lot of non-League away grounds is that you are mixed in with the home fans. So, it is rather impolite to be vociferously vocal in favour of the away team. So, on occasions I restrained myself, but on others I thought, sod it, and shouted with the same vigour that I always do.

After a tense but largely uneventful first half, littered with Harborough set pieces and midfield battles, I clapped off the Yeltz. A young, well-to-do looking young lady, sitting immediately in front of us, must have taken exception to the loudness of my clapping, as she turned round and stared at me disparagingly. For a moment, I thought I must be at the opera, not a football match. I am not sure what she would think if she stood in front of me on the East Terrace at the Grove, while I bawl and cuss.

If the first half was uneventful, the second period began with a bang. For the first time in the contest an experienced Harborough back line allowed KD in behind them. His shot forced a save from the keeper Elliott Taylor. But first to follow up was the quicksilver Conor Tee, who made no mistake dispatching the ball into the net, for his 13th goal of the season. 1-0 to the Yeltz.

Packed in by the home fans, my politeness went completely out of the window, as I stood up, and screamed at the top of my voice, "F*cking get in there!!!" I do not know if I influenced Tom Cartwright's commentary on Yeltz TV, as he was sitting not far from

Kenny and I. But when I watched the highlights back later, he used the very same words – without the expletive, of course.

The game reverted to the tightness of the first half, but Harborough grew more into it and started to push for the equaliser. But they found clear cut chances hard to come by. Then with about 10 minutes left KD managed to wriggle away from the last defender, and his pace took him clear. But it seemed like he was not sure whether to pass to Conor Tee or go for goal himself. His hesitancy was costly, and the golden chance to go 2-0 up was lost.

After that it just seemed like a case of keeping the clean sheet and holding on to the 3 points. But with 5 minutes to go, disaster struck when Jutorre Burgess hit an equaliser for the home side. 1-1. There can be few more dispiriting feelings than being surrounded by opposition fans celebrating an important goal. They were respectful, but of course jubilant.

Harborough had their tails up in front of a big crowd, with minutes to go. So, Russ Penn sensibly brought on Wollacott and Mitchell, defenders, to shore things up and protect the point.

But deep, deep, into stoppage time we got a corner, and I dared to think, "We could snatch the win." After the ball was partly cleared, Parker helped it back into the box and Wynter threw himself at the ball and headed it to KD. KD was 6 yards out, and he swivelled with the goal gaping, and he could do nothing else but score. He missed. KD shot wide, and the chance was gone. Kenny and I were in utter disbelief. It just seemed impossible to miss, especially with KD being our brilliant top scorer. But we knew that nobody would be more gutted than him.

At the final whistle honours were even at 1-1, and on balance it was probably a fair result. Though we should have won it at the death. With Telford and Bedford winning, we are now joint 2nd. Bedford are top and we have the same points and goal difference as Telford.

Sadly, there was some minor infringements between opposing supporters late in the second half. I cannot say for sure what went on, but from video footage I've seen, it looked like mostly very young, misguided teenagers trying, and failing, to look like hard men. When Harborough fans approached Yeltz supporters, the latter sang, "Sit down and behave yourself!" It was all very unfortunate, but credit to the Harborough stewards who dealt with the incident quickly. Yeltz fans on the road have a reputation of being noisy but jolly and good-natured, and generally well received. Especially because of the additional gate receipts and bar takings that we bring. And we do not want that reputation to change.

On the drive home from Leicestershire, Kenny and I tried to divert our attention to other things, but ultimately, we kept coming back to KD's missed chance. It was inescapable. If only, if only, if only. In the grand scheme of things, we hope this proves to be a good point on the road against a top 5 side. Only time will tell. But for now, if that missed chance is haunting me, for poor KD it must be a Hammer House of Horrors

April

Saturday 5 April 2025, St Ives Town Vs Halesowen Town FC - Southern League Premier Central

At points in the season, supporting and being passionate about 2 teams brings with it dilemmas about which game to go to. The Yeltz's league title push and Villa's uncharacteristic FA Cup run to the semi-final have converged to produce the biggest dilemma yet. As both semi-finals are now played at Wembley, one is played on Saturday, and one on Sunday, on the same weekend in April. Villa's one against Crystal Palace has been fixed for Saturday 26 April. This day also happens to be Yeltz's last league game of the season, away at Stamford.

I cannot be in 2 places at once, so one of the games will have to give. If Yeltz have a chance of winning the league at Stamford it makes that game unmissable. I guess that if Villa win the semi-final, I'll be happy because I can go to the final. And if they lose, I will not have missed anything. I will just have to see what transpires in the coming matches.

Less of a dilemma, but a troubling one nonetheless, was which game to go to today. St Ives Town Vs Yeltz, or Villa Vs Nottingham Forest. Both games have great importance for my clubs, with Yeltz striving to be champions, and Villa hoping for a Champions League spot.

Given a simple choice, I would have headed to Cambridgeshire to cheer on the Yeltz. But ultimately my loyalties do not primarily lie with the Yeltz or Villa –

they lie with Kenny. And I know he preferred to go to the Villa game. I get it because when you are a young man the glitz of the topflight seems a lot more appealing – I was the same at Kenny's age. But for me, as I advance more into middle age, the balance is unstoppably tipping more towards my love affair with my hometown non-League club.

With Stourbridge FC's plight over their ground, some of their fans are calling on England and Real Madrid star Jude Bellingham to help, with it being his hometown club. Jude's Dad, Mark, played for the Glassboys, and Jude himself played for the junior team. It will be interesting to see if this leads to anything.

By coincidence, just this week I found out about the Premier League Stadium Fund. The fund provides grants to fund ground improvements for non-League clubs. In the spirit of glasnost, I emailed Stourbridge FC officials to let them know about the fund, in case it can help them. I've had no reply to my email. Maybe they are too busy trying to contact Jude Bellingham. I emailed Yeltz chairman, Keith McKenna, to let him know about the fund too – he did reply, thanking me and saying he's on it.

Stourbridge FC officials have probably not slept well for a while, given the issues with the War Memorial Ground. But they are not the only ones. With nerves over the Yeltz's league run in getting the better of me, I found sleep hard to come by this week. I have tossed and turned with fixtures, stats, league tables, and permutations racing through my head at night. I have tried to calm myself to sleep with the Russ Penn mantra: 'Take one game at a time.' But my thoughts have still run wild.

On the Yeltz forum, spreadsheets have started to emerge about the title challenging teams' respective run ins, and statistical based predictions of the final league table. None I have seen have shown Yeltz as finishing champions. But football is not scientific, which is the very reason we love it.

So, Kenny and I set off for the 5.30 kick-off at Villa Park to the reassuring voices of Matt Ponter, Frank Williams, and Tom Cartwright on Halesowen Town Radio, with live match commentary. It sounded like a tight and even first quarter of the game. When you are away, keeping the home team at bay at 0-0 in the first half can only be a positive thing, as there are no easy games in this league.

Then about 20 minutes in disaster struck. Experienced Yeltz centre-half Jamie Willets fouled Benjamin Mensah, and with the referee deeming the defender to be the last man, the red card was shown. But all did not seem lost with the quality of Ryan Wollacott coming on to slot into the defence, us being on a fine run of form, and St Ives fighting relegation. We still hoped we could get a draw, oh maybe even sneak a win.

According to the commentary, and Ben Ditchfield's subsequent match report, the rest of the game appeared mainly uneventful, with few chances at both ends. The most exciting thing was the Grand National, which took place during the half time break. The second half was an uneasy listen, and tension grew exponentially as the game wore on, especially because at points our title rivals were winning. The final score ended 0-0 in what Russ Penn described as, "really tough conditions", referring to the strong wind.

Penn referred to the draw as a "good point" in his post-match interview, and for good reason: not only did we play for most of the game with 10 men, but additionally, our title rivals of Bedford, Kettering, and Telford only managed draws too. So, at the top end, the league table effectively remains unchanged. We sit in 3rd, 2 points behind table toppers Bedford, and on the same points and goal difference as 2nd place Telford, who go above us on goals scored.

Now, with only 4 games to go, the tension is starting to become unbearable. We host 17th placed Barwell next week, with Bedford, Kettering, and Telford all playing away at Lowestoft (20th), Bishop's Stortford (15th), and Banbury (12th) respectively. It is going to be another rollercoaster of fluctuating emotions and scorelines.

And I am not a fan of rollercoasters. This is because when I was a little kid my brother Warwick and I were on one at Blackpool, and as it was whizzing round, I hit my head on a wooden post. This was in the 1970s, when health and safety was not a top priority. Fortunately, I was wearing a wide brimmed, cowboy style, kiss-me-quick hat, which softened the blow. But if Yeltz fail to get promoted, I do not think a kiss-me-quick hat will ease things. But maybe an Aston Villa FA cup win will. But as of today, glory is possible on both fronts, so for now I'll remain on the rollercoaster.

Saturday 12 April 2025, Halesowen Town FC Vs Barwell FC - Southern League Premier Central

My disrupted sleep continued this week. On Wednesday night I had a nightmare, the theme of which I think was a metaphor for anxiety over Yeltz's title push. I was crossing a rickety bridge over a river by foot, and a second person behind me tried to walk over the bridge too. I told them to wait until I had crossed, as the bridge is unstable, and it might collapse under the weight of two people. But the person kept trying to get on the bridge at the same time as me, and I was terrified it was going to collapse. This surely, is symptomatic of a sense of apprehension that Yeltz's title challenge is going to falter. But the good news is that the bridge did not disintegrate. But only because I woke up screaming, waking an annoyed Lisa in the process.

Phil made the trip from London for this one, and he presented me with a copy of the programme for Dulwich Hamlet's next home game. The reason being, he has recently become the new programme editor for the club. On flicking through the publication, I was impressed by its quality, and it would put a lot of Football League programmes to shame. I said thanks, I'll read it later. But Phil clarified, "Oh, you can't keep it. We only publish 190 copies, so they are in short supply." And he quickly squirrelled it away in a plastic folder.

On the health front, I was finally well enough to watch the game standing on the East Terrace with Kenny,

Phil, and another friend, Kingo. A few weeks ago, I felt like I would not manage that again this season, so being in our familiar spot was a blessing. Especially as it is a great place to banter with the linesman after any dodgy decisions.

Even though we gave Barwell a festive 5-0 thumping at their place, and they are near the relation zone, we knew before this game it would not be easy. Despite their league position Barwell's recent form is good, and they have recruited players since our last meeting. And it turned out to be a challenging game. They were a side far removed from the one who leaked 5 goals at Christmas. They were tough, rugged, and had a steely determination to keep a clean sheet.

As the first half wore on it soon became clear Barwell's defence was going to be harder to penetrate than a tin of corned beef without the key. We had chances though, Wynter and Butterfield had headers saved by keeper Liam Castle. These were followed by a drive by Mini Macca across goal that hit the post and rolled back across the line, into the safety of Castle's arms. We all thought the ball had gone in, but alas it had not.

The second half saw Butterfield drawing a save from Castle with a shot from distance, and time ticked on without us being able to create a clear chance. But all was not lost as Stratford, Kettering, and Telford were all drawing, and inexplicably Bedford were losing at lowly Lowestoft. So, if we could just score a goal, we would catapult above table toppers Bedford to take pole position.

But Barwell held their shape, did not breach, and expertly ran the clock down. I kept saying over and over, "Just one chance!", as if the mantra would somehow lead to the desired outcome. Then in the dying embers of the game, the alert Flanagan took a quick free kick that set Cassidy away down the right. He delivered a perfect low ball across goal with KD, Tee, and Wollacott all bearing down on the 6-yard box. But agonisingly, none of them could touch the ball into the net, and the chance was lost.

The final whistle signalled a 0-0 draw and a monumental feeling of aching frustration, which was difficult to bear. Then the killer blow followed – Bedford, who had pulled the score back to 2-2 at Lowestoft, had snatched a last-minute winner. Kettering won too. This leaves us 4 points behind leaders Bedford, one behind 2nd place Kettering, and on the same points as 3rd placed Telford, but with worse goal difference.

With only 3 games left, it feels like the title is out of our grasp, and that dream is over. We now must concentrate on trying to secure 2nd or 3rd place, which means home advantage in a play-off semi-final tie.

In Roberto's Bar, I was shell shocked, numb, lifeless. Though, I could just about lift my pint to my lips. Kenny and I were pretty quiet. I had dreamt of us Yeltzfolk celebrating an historic title win in the sunshine at Stamford. But it serves me right, as I am long enough in the tooth to know that in football you should never look further ahead than the next game.

In times of despondency, you look to the manager for inspiration. And Russ Penn delivered it in his post-match interview. He was calm, positive, and retained his focus and determination to get the club promoted: "Frustrated is the word, but I'm still pleased, it's a good point." The subtext to his interview was, "Ok, if we cannot win league, then we will just have to win the play-offs."

Hopefully, Penn's reassuring calmness will lead me to sleeping better this week. I need to re-energise ahead of a bumper football schedule next weekend, a Bank holiday.

Saturday 19 April 2025, Leiston FC Vs Halesowen Town FC - Southern League Premier Central

With yesterday being Good Friday, some games in this division were played, with the remaining fixtures today. Of the promotion candidates, only Telford and Harborough had games, the former at home to Lowestoft, and the latter away to Redditch. Yeltz fans were particularly hoping against hope that already relegated Lowestoft would do us a favour. But it was disappointing to see that Telford scored in the first minute, and they continued to do so for the rest of the game. They won by a goal difference boosting 7-1.

Harborough won 1-0, pushing them up to 5th, 4 points behind us in 4th. So, ahead of this one, a win for us was crucial. 3 points should be enough to guarantee a play-off place, and we'd be level pegging on points with Telford ahead of our game with them at the Grove on Monday.

Yesterday, it was great to see that Kidderminster Harriers, my footballing mistress, won, and Scunthorpe lost, meaning that Kiddy are now table toppers with 2 to play. Like every good mistress, Kidderminster is far enough away from home to be out of sight, but close enough to travel to when needed. But I definitely do not want a Kiddy with my mistress, not at this stage in life.

None of my Yeltz mates were going to this game, and it understandable with it being an 8 hour round trip, one of the furthest. And Kenny is away in Tenerife. So, I chose to go to Villa Vs Newcastle at 5.30, an exciting prospect, with both teams chasing Champions League spots.

With Villa kicking off at teatime, it meant I was able to listen to the Yeltz commentary on Halesowen Town Radio. The picture painted in the early parts of the game by commentators Tom Cartwright, Matt Ponter, Frank Williams, and Nick Morgan gave me full confidence that we were going to win this one. And fortunately, that is the way it turned out.

In short, this 3-0 win, at the Victory Road ground, was the Conor Tee show. The Industrious and skilful wide man continued his season's sparkling form by scoring 2 and setting up the other for KD. Our first goal saw Tee deliver one of the crosses of the season, which had the word 'goal' written all over it. KD got on the end of it to poke it home on 35 minutes, for his 26th of the campaign.

Tee then sealed the game with a brace of goals in a 10-minute spell, starting on the hour. His first was a cracker, a curling free kick from 30 yards out. He then confidently converted a penalty after a Leiston player handled in the box, notching his 15th of the season. Tee has been nothing short of magnificent since game one, and must be a strong contender for player of the season.

The Yeltz faithful who made the arduous trip to deepest Suffolk were not only rewarded with 3 points and a convincing performance. The Yeltz players shook the hands off every single one of them, and chairman Keith McKenna even went on to the fan's coach to thank them for their superb support. It's one thing players or managers saying they value the fans, but it's another when the players, staff, and Chairman give their heartfelt thanks with gestures like these. Because it means the world to the supporters to be properly appreciated.

The win secured our play-off place and takes us into Monday's crucial home game with Telford in confident mood. Ideally, we need to gain a home play-off tie by finishing 2nd or 3rd, and a win over Telford will go a long way to achieving that. Bedford and Kettering won today too. So, we remain 4th, 4 points behind top side Bedford, 1 point behind Kettering, and on the same points as Telford, who have a +3 superior goal difference.

I went into Villa Park in jubilant mood, and it continued as Villa beat Newcastle by a whopping 4-1. And it could have been by more. With Kenny still holidaying abroad, my brother Warwick joined me in the Holte End, instead of taking up his normal seat in the Trinity Road Stand. It stuck me that it was the first time we had stood on the Holte End together since we were young men. So, it was great to share the victory's elation with my older sibling. It made me think of childhood and the days when my footballing odyssey began.

Now, having played over 1,000 games, and watched too many to count, when football goes well it still has the capacity to make me glow with blissful joy.

Monday 21 April 2025, Halesowen Town FC Vs AFC Telford United - Southern League Premier Central

Shortly after this game, the good news arrived that our bitter rivals Stourbridge FC have come to an agreement with the Southern League, meaning they can use their War Memorial Ground next season. In a statement on X SFC said, "We hope this will give us the required time to complete the works required to secure the future of the ground."

The timing of the announcement was interesting. It was Stourbridge's last home game of the campaign today. It could be said their marketing of the game gave the impression they would not be able to play at the War Memorial Ground next season. On X they encouraged fans to turn up for 'Our farewell to the WMAG as we know it', 'Its final show', and 'to say goodbye to the WMAG in its current guise.'

In hindsight, the phrases 'as we know it' and 'in its current guise' were important, given the subsequent announcement. SFC's marketing helped get 1,282 through the turnstiles, a bumper crowd for them. They were playing Bromsgrove though, a local team.

The Glassboys having reached a short-term resolution to their issues is positive not only for them. It also means the number 9 derby will be contested next season, which is pleasing for us Yeltz fans. But our ticket allocation for the away game could potentially be lower than this season's 450.

Tickets for this Yeltz game were less scarce, but you needed one to watch this showdown, with it being an all-ticket game. Unlike other away fans, except Stourbridge, Telford supporters are usually segregated for this fixture. It made for a special bank holiday atmosphere at the Grove for the 2,374 in attendance, with both sets of fans passionately backing their teams.

Although I now thankfully feel relatively well, we were back to sitting in the Harry Rudge stand to watch this one. Like Michael Corleone in *The Godfather Part III* I felt like saying, "Just when I thought I was out, they pull me back in." Us sitting down was due to Kenny. He bashed his knee holidaying in Tenerife and is on crutches.

Fortunately, none of the Yeltz players are on crutches, or victims of less serious injuries, so Russ Penn had a full squad to pick from. The first name on the team sheet is always our experienced and reliable keeper, Dan Platt. This was a special day for him as his 336th appearance meant he has now turned our more times than any other Yeltz goalkeeper. He has overtaken the FA Vase winning legend Phil Coldicott. Phil was also at the game as players from the FA Vase team were cheered at half-time. This was to mark the 40th

anniversary of our first Vase win in 1985. There was a presentation for Platty before kick-off.

Our strong side started well enough, in what was a tense and tight game between two evenly matched teams. But it was Telford who took the lead on 20 minutes through a Dylan Allen-Hadley tap in, with their first serious attack of the game. It was a scrappy goal to concede.

Then we then slowly grew into the game, and built increasing momentum, but we could not find the finishing touch. But that quickly changed just after the break, when Mini-Macca slung in a delightful far post cross for KD to head in. The goal not only elicited feelings of great joy, but it released an almost overwhelming pent-up tension that had been building during the tight, competitive game. At that point, I was quietly confident we could win.

But Telford dug in, and as the game wore on, they seemed happy to protect their point. We had a few half chances but were unable to convert. The ref's full-time whistle confirmed the 1-1 draw and that our title chances were now mathematically at an end, as Bedford won. Kettering won too, so we remain 4th, and with only one game to go, the best we can hope for now is 3rd. To achieve that we need to better Telford's result, or if we both win, to better their superior +3 goal difference.

With an away semi-final now a distinct possibility, I reserved a place on the supporters' coach, just in case. The result also means I will be on another coach next Saturday – Kenny and I will be travelling to

Wembley for Villa's FA Cup semi-final. As Yeltz cannot win the league at Stamford, it is the obvious option.

With the Vase anniversary celebration, Platty's achievement, and the tense, pulsating game in front of a big crowd, it was a dramatic, poignant, and stirring day. But with the game ending in a draw, I found it hard to get my emotions in order.

But a grounded Russ Penn was upbeat: "Today was a great advert for the league. We had two teams going at it for 90 minutes plus stoppage time, and the crowd made it for me. I think we deserved to get the win, but we never looked like losing and have gone 12 unbeaten.....the whole team was fantastic...... we will have a large travelling support [*going to Stamford*] and will look to come back to The Grove a week on Wednesday."

Saturday 26 April 2025, Stamford AFC Vs Halesowen Town FC - Southern League Premier Central

In his pre-match interview on Thursday, ahead of their crucial away game at Southport, Kidderminster Harrier's manager Phil Brown said, "Football is fantastic, it really is." And many times this season I have shared his sentiments. But today was not one of them. It was almost a complete disaster.

Last Wednesday I should have known that the omens for today were bad. Lisa and I went to watch a different live sport – horse racing at Ludlow. The horses that I bet on in the first 3 races got nowhere near making a place. The 4th race only had 5 runners, and the favourite was at such short odds, that the winner looked like a foregone conclusion. So, I decided not to place a bet, and neither did Lisa. But we agreed to pick a horse each 'just for fun', both outsiders. Predictably, my horse won the race. Picking a horse without betting on it was an unforgivable amateur error, and I chided myself for my stupidity. It was far from fun. Of course, the horses I bet on in the last two races were failures too.

Phil Brown's experiences today would not have been fun either. In the last game of their regular season, Kiddy simply needed to win away at lowly Southport to clinch the league title. But Brown probably thought that football is less than fantastic, as they lost 2-1, in what sounded like a very poor, flat performance. Kiddy now seek promotion to the National League via the alternative route of the play-offs.

In Villa's FA Cup semi-final at Wembley Vs Crystal Palace, a tea-time kick off, things got worse. Not only did we lose 3-0, but we also played awfully too. Kenny and I had high hopes we would make it to the final and go on to win the Cup. Not only was I desperate for Villa to fulfil my lifelong dream of winning the Cup, but it would have been lovely for Kenny and I to share our first trophy win together too.

The footballing cliché is that Wembley is the worst place to lose. I do not necessarily subscribe to that, as dedicated football fans can feel devastated losing a big game at any football ground. But Wembley is a bad place to taste defeat because I find the whole experience of going there relatively unpleasant, even though it is an impressive stadium. I dislike the busy and congested nature of the outside of the ground, the ludicrous prices for everything, and the hassle of travelling to the location.

When talk first emerged of Wembley being redeveloped in the 1990's, I was an advocate of building a new national football stadium at an accessible site in the Midlands. But to some decision makers, it seems like the world does not exist outside the capital.

While waiting for our emotionally crushing semi-final to kick-off, Kenny and I focussed on the Yeltz game. The best we could do to follow it, and Telford's game, was on social media and another football app we use. The headline from the team news was there was no KD or Todd Parker in the squad. Russ Penn later said they had been left out because of minor injuries.

The first click to check the scoreline was not a good one. It told us that Yeltz were 1-0 down after just one minute, to a James Blunden goal. But just 9 minutes later, the ever-reliable Conor Tee hit back with another long-range free kick, which was fumbled into the net by keeper Tom Jackson. 1-1.

We were delighted to see that mid-table Royston were winning 1-0 at Telford. So, at this stage we were above Telford, at 3rd in the table. If that stayed the same, our play-off tie against Telford would be at the Grove.

Stamford quickly retook the lead, a stunning strike by Charlie Marzano doing the damage. It was reported that we were lucky not to go further behind. But just before the break we had the chance to equalise. Jamie Willets' goal bound header was handled by a Stamford defender, resulting in a penalty. Up stepped Tee, who had scored all his previous 3 penalties this season - and hit the post. But another effort by Willets on the hour proved more decisive, as he volleyed in at the back post following a corner. 2-2.

The next half an hour or so saw me repeatedly refreshing my phone for score updates. But the more Wembley filled up, the less signal I had. The games wore on, with the scores still being 2-2, and 0-1 at Telford. We either needed the scores to stay the same, or even better, for Yeltz to get a winner. Then, even if Telford equalised, we would still finish 3rd.

With 5 minutes of the games to go I frantically and obsessively refreshed my phone, praying for a Yeltz goal, a Royston clean sheet, or both. It was beyond agonising. Finally, at least 10 minutes after the Yeltz game must have finished, my phone showed a 'FT' after the score, confirming a 2-2 draw. But no matter how many times I refreshed my phone, I could not get confirmation that the Telford game was over. Eventually, the 'FT' displayed on the Telford score too - but there was an unwanted additional piece of information. Frustratingly, Telford had scored a later equaliser to force a draw.

With both the Yeltz and Telford drawing, this meant they remained 3rd and us $4^{th.}$ This means we must travel to Telford's New Bucks Head stadium on Wednesday for the play-off semi-final. I thought to myself that, ok, all is not lost. Even though we will be away from home, we can still win the game. Plus,

Kenny and I now have Villa's semi-final to look forward to.....

With Villa losing the game in such bitterly disappointing fashion, Yeltz's play-off on Wednesday has taken on even more significance for me. If Yeltz lose, it will be unbearable. But what can I do to help Yeltz win? Well for a start, I can refrain from placing a bet on them.

Wednesday 30 April 2025, AFC Telford United Vs Halesowen Town FC - Southern League Premier Central play-off semi-final

My feeling before this game was one more of hope than expectation. This was because I was still down after Villa's heartbreaking semi-final defeat at Wembley on Saturday. Also, I have unpleasant memories of the last time Yeltz played at the New Buck's Head Stadium, on Boxing Day, as we came away with nothing after a 2-0 defeat. Though I did retain full faith in the team, particularly as we were on a 13-match unbeaten run. So, my reservations were more down to me than the reality of the situation.

Out of those 13 matches 6 were draws, with 5 of those coming in the 6 games prior to tonight. So, recently we have found it harder to kill teams off, but equally they are not killing us off either. But Telford were in much the same position – clocking up 10 draws in a 16-game unbeaten run.

I told myself that in a one-off game anything can happen. And one thing is for sure, I knew all the players would be 100% focused and determined. If we played at our best, we stood a great chance of winning.

But I knew that if we lost tonight, it would be shattering, especially coming off the back of the anguish last Saturday. I decided to plan ahead and get myself a little insurance policy. If Yeltz's season ends tonight, I knew that if I had another potential success to look forward to, it would take the edge off. So, I bought Kenny and I tickets for Kidderminster Harriers' play-off semi-final game at Aggborough on Sunday, against Chester.

But I knew that my insurance policy could potentially pose a problem ahead of the forthcoming Bank Holiday weekend. I knew if Yeltz won tonight, their play-off final will be on Monday. So, that could mean I will be at Villa Park on Saturday, Aggborough on Sunday, and at the Yeltz game on Monday, which I am sure Lisa will be understandably less than pleased about.

Things did not start well this evening, because the leader lost his way. Not Russ Penn, but the coach driver. On arriving at the New Bucks Head at 6.30 he took a wrong turn. This led to a 30-minute detour before arriving back at the stadium. This included a police escort to get the vehicle out of an estate of narrow streets, which were wholly unsuitable for a coach.

With 3,204 inside the New Bucks Head creating a great atmosphere, with about 800 hundred from Halesowen, it had the look and feel of a Football League game. Such is the outstanding depth and quality of the non-League game in this country. It was quite a sight, and I'm sure it would have further inspired both sets of players to want to get promoted, to play in bigger grounds in the Nation League North, some ex-Football League stadiums. It whetted my appetite, for sure.

Predictably, the first quarter of the game was played at a high tempo and was scrappy. Both teams played relatively risk-free football and were unable to put together decent attacking moves. But then on 22 minutes the Yeltz drew first blood. Livewire KD headed in Conor Tee's corner in front of the Telford fans, his 28th of the season. It was an incredible start, but I looked at the clock and thought, this game is going to produce more goals.

We then exerted further pressure on the Telford goal, and we could have scored a 2nd. But the home side grew into the game, and their hunt for an equaliser came to fruition on 42 minutes. Dylan Allen-Hadley found the top right corner of the net from close range after Yeltz failed to clear.

Ok, 1-1 at the break, I thought, we'll take that. Penn can lift the team at half-time, and tweak things, if necessary, for a renewed push in the second half. But Telford were not done, and disastrously they extended their lead to 2-1 just before the break. Pendley scored when we failed to deal with a free kick delivered into the box. Penn now really had to use all his skills and experience to re-energise the team.

At half time I left behind Kev, Sid, and Ade, who I was standing with behind the goal, and switched to a seat in the main stand. I do not know if it was the heat, the stresses and excitement of the game, or both, but the dizziness and symptoms of my neurological condition hit me. I was struggling to stand up, so did the sensible thing, and switched to the stand with seating. Only to bizarrely find Roberto, landlord of my local, sitting in the stand with barman Jacob. Roberto had wangled a hospitality package through a contact.

Yeltz looked to draw level early in the second half, but Telford's defence stood firm, and opportunities were scarce. The play from both sides again became scrappy, and we found it hard to play with the fluidity needed to create a proper chance. At the same time, as we pushed more players forward, we left ourselves open to counter attacks.

On 65 minutes the gaffer decided we needed more attacking impetus, and threw on striker Charlie Wragg, and reverted to a 3-5-2 system. The pacey Wragg had an impact and slowly started to unsettle the home side's back line. But in all honesty, we did not look like scoring.

Then 10 minutes after his introduction, Wragg latched onto a decent cross from the left from Mini Macca and buried his header into the corner. And together with the rest of the Yeltzfolk, I went absolutely crazy. With the momentum of the equaliser, and a riotously vocal away crowd, I could now see us winning the game.

A mere 2 minutes later, a Telford player passed the ball down the heart of our defence - but it was OK, as Ryan Wollacott was there, and he was having a fantastic game. But time stood still when the unfortunate Wollacott made an error, and Matt Stenson ran clear, to slide the ball past Platty. 3-2.

Attacking substitutes of Cameron, Hickman, and Flanagan were all introduced at intervals, but as the minutes wiled away, we could not create that elusive chance. Time ran like sand through my fingers, and in what seemed like the flash of an eye, the 90 minutes were up. Then renewed hope – 6 minutes of stoppage time was announced. We had a flurry of attacking corners and free kicks, but we could not get on the end of them, and Telford held firm.

Then in the last seconds of the game we got a corner. Flanagan frantically rushed to take it, fearing the referee would blow the final whistle. This being the last throw of the dice, even goalkeeper Platty sprinted into the box. Flanagan's corner was cleared but eventually a decent move found Jak Hickman with the ball on the byline, and he delivered one of his trademark crosses. The cross was head height, between the sticks, but beyond the reach of keeper Brandon Hall. Platty got a firm header on the ball, and it was goalward, and going just under the bar. The hearts were in the mouths of everyone in the stadium. Brandon Hall thrust an arm up - and incredibly tipped the ball to safety over the bar.

It was a match winning save. Because immediately after it, the cutting sound of the referee's whistle sounded, to signal our crushed dreams. A season defined by an error at one end, and a world class save at the other. Yeltz players sank dejected to the turf. As Runn Penn said later in his post-match interview, "Football is cruel."

But as the dust started to settle on the pulsating contest, out poured a cascade of mutual love, from the fans to the players and staff, and visa versa. We all knew that the team had tried their absolute utmost, epitomised by our magnificent captain, Ryan Wynter. We had lost the game by a very fine margin. Also, this promotion push was a great improvement on last season's mid-table finish.

Walking back to the supporters' coach, I had a bit of an existential crisis, self-questioning, why do I do this to myself? What is the point of football anyway? But I quickly realised that a large part of the point is electric nights like tonight, which make me feel more alive than ever.

On the coach back from Wembley on Saturday, I was completely desolate. I could see no good in the experience I just had. But tonight was different. The coach was a good spirited Yeltz community, and pride and stoicism were the overriding feelings. I shared a beer with well-known Yeltz character Mankini Dave, and although everybody was disappointed, people quickly started to lighten up. They were my people, my fellow townsfolk, and Yeltz fans, and I felt completely at home.

The spirit of togetherness was embodied by Sheila, who walked up the aisle of the coach with a Tupperware box of varied boiled sweets, or 'suck' as we call them in the Black Country. She offered them to everyone. Sweet was the perfect word for Sheila's kind gesture, one that heartened everyone. It was something that perfectly summed up the beauty and camaraderie of non-League football. The humbug soothed my soul and reminded me of the great warmth and humanity of people.

Before I knew it, the coach arrived back at the Grove at around 11pm. It was late, but after the evening I had experienced, I simply needed a beer. I walked into the town and past Roberto's Bar, but I could see that Toni behind the bar was finishing up. So, I gave her a wave and walked on. Wetherspoons was the only option, so in I went. It was almost as if they knew what I needed, because one of my favourite beers was on the bar, Thornbridge Jaipur. Taking the top off my pint, I saw Kev sitting alone, gesturing me to join him.

The Jaipur, and the game debrief with fellow Yeltzman Kev, was just what I needed, as it perfectly bookended the evening. It allowed me to let go of the defeat's heartache sufficiently to go home and carry on with life.

It was great to see that the outpouring of love for the team continued on social media, often a place for cynicism and backbiting. In his post-match interview, Russ Penn continued to display his drive to get us promoted. He said that after a short break he will quickly start work on preparing for next season. But for the Yeltz, finally, this season is over.

Afterword

I still had my 'insurance policy' game of Kidderminster Harriers FC Vs Chester FC in the National League North play-off semi-final. But like Yeltz's play-off match, and Villa's Cup semi-final, it did not end well.

After taking the lead on 20 minutes, Kiddy were in control. But they were pegged back to 1-1 10 minutes before the break in unfortunate circumstances, with a Chester player clearly offside. This poor decision by the linesman seemed to alter the whole course of the game. In the 2nd half Kiddy could not quite find the same rhythm, and in the 82nd minute Chester took the lead. The game ended 2-1 to the visitors, and signalled the end of Harriers' promotion hopes. In these one-off games of jeopardy, small margins, like the absence of a linesman's flag, can make all the difference.

Unlike at the end of the Yeltz's play-off match, the atmosphere at Aggborough at the final whistle was desolate. The collective feeling in the stadium did not stray beyond that of total dismay. You could almost touch the disappointment. Kiddy were one of the promotion favourites, a professional club in a league of mostly part timers. This was compounded by their failure on the season's final day, when a win would have guaranteed the title.

I felt sorrowful and a sense of anticlimax, but to not the same degree as following the Yeltz and Villa games. So, it was almost like I was weaning myself off these emotions.

A few days later Phil Brown and assistant Neil McDonald were, somewhat surprisingly, sacked. It saddened me, partly because Brown brought colour and entertainment to his post and pre-match press conferences. The overarching feeling on Harriers' social media was that Kiddy fans were surprised and disappointed by the move. It will not only be interesting to see who the new manager is, but also whether at 65 Brown will again step into the arena of football management. I guess most managers finish their career on the sour note of a sacking. It's an odd and unique profession.

Brown has been replaced by Adam Murray, a 43-year-old, with an impressive managerial CV. It includes management and coaching at clubs including Mansfield Town, Barnsley, Cheltenham, West Bromwich Albion, Beşiktaş, AFC Fylde, and Eastbourne. As a player he made over 500 appearances in the Premier League, EFL, and non-League.

Rushall Olympic ended up at the other end of the National League North table, 3rd from bottom. So, after a plucky effort, that included wins over big sides like Kidderminster and Scunthorpe, they were relegated. Richard Sneekes stood down as manager, to take up a different position within the club, and has been replaced by Rushall favourite Ian Long.

There has been no such managerial change at the Grove. Once the obligatory break is over, Russ Penn will go full steam ahead with planning next season's promotion challenge. The general mood seems to be that the club's target at the start of the season was to finish in the play-off places, as a minimum. And we achieved that, so Penn has the overall support of the fans to go again.

Telford won 4-2 at Kettering in the Southern League Premier Division Central play-off final, to progress to the National League North. Bedford Town were promoted as Champions, also oddly to the National League North. Barwell, Lowestoft, Hitchin, and Biggleswade were relegated. Though Barwell later got a reprieve because Farsely Celtic, who were relegated from the National League North, lost their licence to play in steps 1-4, so were relegated to Step 5.

As for Villa, a top 6 finish guaranteed a place in the Europa League for next season. The way the final day results turned out, a draw would have guaranteed a top 5 place, and Champions League qualification. But Villa lost 2-0 at Manchester United in their final game, after having a controversial goal ruled out at 0-0 with 10 men.

So, overall, a season that at one point, promised promotion for Yeltz and Kiddy, and the FA Cup for Villa, delivered none of things, even though it was one helluva ride. But in football, there is always next season.

Halesowen Town FC statistics, season 2024/25

Halesowen Town awards winners for 2024/25 Season:

- Top goal scorer: Kieren Donnelly - 28 Goals.
- Player's player of the season: Conor Tee.
- Manager Russ Penn's player of the season: Josh Smile.
- Chairman Keith McKenna's player of the season: Conor Tee.
- President Colin Brookes's player of the season: Ryan Wynter.
- Spitfire supporter's player of the season: Kieren Donnelly.
- Radio Halesowen Town's player of the season: Josh Smile.
- Club person of the year: Jackie Brookes.
- Fans of the year: Gary and Ryan Winter.
- Volunteers of the year: Julie and Terry.
- Daniel Platt received a goalkeeper's shirt for 336 appearances for the club, which is a club record for a keeper.

Pre-season results

- 13.07.24. Tamworth FC. H. 2-2. Wynter, Tee.
- 16.07.24: Worcester City FC. A. Won 3-0. Manning, Flanagan, and Donnelly.
- 20.07.24: Rugby Town. A. Won 1-0. Yussuf
- 23.07.24: Solihull Moors. H. Lost 3-0.
- 27.07.24: Hereford. H. 2-2. Triallist and Manning.

- 03.08.24: Leamington. A. Lost 1-0.

Season proper results

1. Sat 10 Aug 24. H. Kettering Town. Lg. Won. 2-1. Flanagan (pen), Manning. 1,216.
2. Mon 12 Aug. A. Redditch United. Lg. 2-2. Wynter, Donnelly. Manning sent off (2 yellows). 933.
3. Sat 17 Aug 24. H. Bedford Town. Lg. Lost 4-1. Yussuf. 902.
4. Sat 24 Aug 24. H St Ives Town. Lg. Won 1-0. Tee. 749.
5. Mon 26 Aug 24. A. Bromsgrove Sporting. Lg. Won 2-1. Kelly, Donnelly. 1,310.
6. Sat 31 Aug 24. A. Redditch United. Lost 3-2. FA Cup Q1. Donnelly 2. Yussuf sent-off (straight red) 688.
7. Sat 7 Sept 24. H. Leiston. Lg. 1-1. Luisiana. 1,203.
8. Tues 10 Sept 24. A. Banbury United. Lg. Won 1-0. Boothe. 568.
9. Sat 14 Sept 24. A. Alvechurch. Lg. Lost 1-0. 704.
10. Sat 21 Sept 24. H. Hitchin Town. Lg. Lost 4-0. 716.
11. Tues 24 Sept 24. H. Harborough Town. Lg. Won 1-0. Donnelly. 615.
12. Sat 28 Sept 24. H. Stratford Town. Lg. Lost 3-2. Tee, Donnelly. 1,003.
13. Sat 5 Oct 24. A. Redditch United. FA Trophy 3Q. Won 3-0. Donnelly, Manning, Ponticelli. 476.
14. Sat 19 Oct 24. A. Bishop Stortford. Lg. Won 2-1. Donnelly 2. 531.

15. Sat 26 Oct 24. H. Congleton Town. FA Trophy 1. Won 4-1. Tee, Ceesay, Manning, Ponticelli (pen). 808.
16. Sat 2 Nov 24. H. Spalding United. Lg. Won 2-1. Ponticelli, Donnelly. 1,035.
17. Tues 5 Nov 24. A. Lowestoft Town. Lg. Won 5-0. Donnelly 3, Ponticelli, Tee. 354
18. Sat 9 Nov 24. H. AFC Sudbury. Lg. Won 3-1. Ponticelli 2, Donnelly. Manning sent-off (2 yellows), Donnelly sent-off (2 yellows – 1 on the pitch, 1 subsequently on the bench). 1,021.
19. Sat 16 Nov. A. Kidderminster Harriers. FA Trophy 2. Lost 2-1. Ponticelli. 3,884 (1,442 Halesowen).
20. Sat 23 Nov 24. H. Biggleswade Town. Lg. Won 3-1. Donnelly, Ponticelli, Tee (pen). 703
21. Sat 30 Nov 24. A. Stourbridge. Lg. 2-2. Donnelly 2. 1,834.
22. Tues 3 Dec 24. A. Leamington. Birmingham Senior Cup 2nd round. 1-1. Ryan Fletcher. Lost 6-5 on pens.
23. Tues 10 Dec 24. A. Royston Town. Lg. Lost 1-0. 237. Wynter sent-off, straight red.
24. Sat 14 Dec 24. A. Barwell. Lg. Won 5-0. Wynter 2, Ceesay, Donnelly, Tee. 387.
25. Sat 21 Dec 24. H. Redditch United. Lg. Won 2-1. Wollacott, Tee. 1,259.
26. Thurs 26 Dec 24. A. AFC Telford United. Lg. Lost 2-0. 2,047 (339 Yeltz)
27. Sat 28 Dec 24. Bedford Town. A. Lg. Lost 3-1. Tee (pen.) Ceesay sent-off (2 yellow cards) 1,028.
28. Wed 1 Jan 25. H. Bromsgrove Sporting. Lg. Lost 2-0. 1,503

29. Tues 14 Jan 25. H. Stamford. Lg. Won 2-0. Smile, Tee (pen). 570.
30. Sat 18 Jan 25. A. AFC Sudbury. Lg. 0-0. 320
31. Tues 21 Jan 25. H. Royston Town. Lg. Won 2-0. Tee 2. 512.
32. Sat 25 Jan 25. A. Stratford Town. Lg. Lost 2-0. 1,427.
33. Sat 1 Feb 25. H. Bishops Stortford. Lg. Won 4-0. Donnelly 2, Wollacott, Manning. 1,147.
34. Sat 8 Feb 25. A. Spalding United. Lg. Lost 2-0. 516
35. Sat 15 Feb 25. H. Alvechurch. Lg. 2-2. Donnelly, Tee. Wynter sent-off, straight red. 923
36. Sat 22 Feb 25. H. Stourbridge. Lg. Won 3-1. Donnelly 2, Wragg. 3,043.
37. Tues 25 Feb 25. A. Kettering Town. Lg. 0-0. 996.
38. Sat 1 Mar 25. A. Biggleswade Town. Lg. Won 1-0. Cameron. 190.
39. Sat 8 Mar 25. H. Banbury United. Lg. Won.1-0. Donnelly. 1,046.
40. Sat 15 Mar 25. A Hitchin Town. Lg. Won 2-1. Tee, Donnelly. 702.
41. Sat 22 Mar 25. H. Lowestoft Town. Lg. Won 3-1. Wynter, Cameron, Manning. 1,584.
42. Sat 29 Mar 25. A. Harborough Town. Lg. Drew 1-1. Tee. 1,002.
43. Sat 5 Apr 25. A. St Ives Town. Lg. 0-0. 399.
44. Sat 12 Apr 25. H. Barwell. Lg. 0-0. 1,241.
45. Sat 19 Apr. 25. A. Leiston FC. Lg. Won 3-0. Tee 2, Donnelly. 249.
46. Mon 21 Apr 25. H. AFC Telford United. Lg. 1-1. Donnelly. 2,374.

47. Sat 26 Apr 25. A. Stamford AFC. Lg. 2-2. Tee, Willets. 967.
48. Wed 30 April. A. AFC Telford United. SLC play-off SF. Lost 3-2. Donnelly, Wragg. 3,204.

Southern League Premier Central, final league table

		P	Pts	GD	
1.	Bedford Town	42	82	+21	C
2.	Kettering Town	42	77	+29	
3.	AFC Telford United	42	74	+22	P
4.	Halesowen Town	42	74	+19	
5.	Harborough Town	42	71	+23	
6.	Stamford	42	69	+2	
7.	Spalding United	42	68	+16	
8.	Stratford Town	42	67	+17	
9.	Stourbridge	42	63	+10	
10.	Leiston	42	60	-2	
11.	Royston Town	42	57	+2	
12.	Banbury United	42	57	0	
13.	Alvechurch	42	56	+3	
14.	Bromsgrove Sporting	42	51	-4	
15.	Bishop's Stortford	42	51	-10	
16.	St Ives Town	42	50	-2	
17.	AFC Sudbury	42	50	-5	
18.	Redditch United	42	49	-8	
19.	Barwell	42	46	-19	
20.	Lowestoft Town	42	37	-51	R
21.	Hitchin Town	42	34	-30	R
22.	Biggleswade Town	42	28	-33	R

Printed in Dunstable, United Kingdom